NEW RECIPES FOR FERMENTED FOODS 2022

100 RECIPES FOR A HEALTHY GUT

THOMAS PRICE

All rights reserved.

Disclaimer

The information contained in this eBook is meant to serve as a comprehensive collection of strategies that the author of this eBook has done research about. Summaries, strategies, tips and tricks are only recommendation by the author, and reading this eBook will not guarantee that one's results will exactly mirror the author's results. The author of the eBook has made all reasonable effort to provide current and accurate information for the readers of the eBook. The author and its associates will not be held liable for any unintentional error or omissions that may be found. The material in the eBook may include information by third parties. Third party materials comprise of opinions expressed by their owners. As such, the author of the eBook does not assume responsibility or liability for any third party material or opinions. Whether because of the progression of the internet, or the unforeseen changes in company policy and editorial submission guidelines, what is stated as fact at the time of this writing may become outdated or inapplicable later.

The eBook is copyright © 2022 with all rights reserved. It is illegal to redistribute, copy, or create derivative work from this eBook whole or in part. No parts of this report may be reproduced or retransmitted in any reproduced or retransmitted in any forms whatsoever without the writing expressed and signed permission from the author.

TABLE OF CONTENTS

TABLE OF CONTENTS..4

INTRODUCTION..8
    WHAT IS FERMENTATION?...9
    IS FERMENTATION SAFE?..10
    BEST FERMENTED FOODS...12

FERMENTED SAUCES..14
    1. LOUISIANA-STYLE HOT SAUCE..15
    2. CHIMICHURRI VERDE..18
    3. AJÍ AMARILLO SAUCE..21
    4. GARLICKY GREEN CHILI SAUCE..24
    5. CHIPOTLE HOT SAUCE...27
    6. AJÍ PICANTE...30

FERMENTED DAIRY...37
    8. TRADITIONAL VEGAN YOGURT...38
    9. CULTURED COCONUT CREAM..41
    10. HOMEMADE FERMENTED YOGURT......................................45
    11. DAIRY-FREE CREAM..48
    12. GLUTEN-FREE, DAIRY-FREE REJUVELAC.............................51
    13. YOGURT CHEESE..54
    14. ALMOND FARMER'S CHEESE...57
    15. WALNUT THYME CHEESE...61
    16. BRACOTTA CHEESE..64
    17. MACADAMIA CREAM CHEESE...67
    18. AGED SMOKED CHEESE..70
    19. AGED MISO CHEESE..73
    20. AGED SAVORELLA CHEESE...76

SAUERKRAUT & PICKLES..................................79

21. Basic Sauerkraut..................................80
22. Spiced Sauerkraut.................................83
23. Five-Minute Broccoli Sauerkraut...................87
24. Pineapple Sauerkraut..............................91
25. Purple Sauerkraut.................................95
26. Spicy Dill Fermented Pickles......................99
27. Salvadoran Salsa.................................103
28. Star Anise Carrots...............................106
29. Cultured Onions..................................109
30. Red-Hot Hot Sauce................................112
31. Fermented Chopped Salad..........................115
32. Dill Cucumber Pickle Bites.......................118
33. Zucchini Pickles.................................121
34. Taco Pickles....................................124
35. White Kimchi....................................127

FRUIT CULTURES & VINEGARS..........................131

36. Cultured Spicy Peach Chutney....................132
37. Sweet Vanilla Peaches...........................135
38. Crabapple Vinegar...............................137
39. Apple Vinegar..................................140
40. Pineapple Vinegar..............................144

CULTURED BEVERAGES................................147

41. Vegan Kefir....................................148
42. Black Tea Kombucha.............................151
43. African Red Tea Kombucha.......................155
44. Cultured Bloody Mary...........................159

FERMENTED DESSERTS...............................162

45. Tzatziki......................................163
46. Creamy French Onion Dip........................166
47. Green Salad with Peaches & Chèvre..............169

48. Coconut Cream Cheese..172
49. Pear Crêpes with Macadamia Cheese.....................175
50. Gingerbread Cookie Ice Cream Sandwiches............179
51. Cultured Vanilla Ice Cream......................................182
52. Pumpkin Pie Ice Cream..185
53. Black Cherry Ice Cream..188
54. Orange Creamsicle Cheesecake...............................191
55. Pomegranate Cheesecake...194
56. Blackberry Cheesecake..198

FERMENTED VEGGIES..202

57. Dill pickles..203
58. Sauerkraut...207
59. Bread-and-butter pickles...210
60. Dill pickles..213
61. Sweet gherkin pickles..216
62. 14-Day sweet pickles..220
63. Quick sweet pickles..223
64. Pickled asparagus..226
65. Pickled dilled beans...229
66. Pickled three-bean salad...232
67. Pickled beets..235
68. Pickled carrots..238
69. Pickled cauliflower/Brussels..................................241
70. Chayote and jicama slaw...244
71. Bread-and-butter pickled jicama...........................247
72. Marinated whole mushrooms.................................250
73. Pickled dilled okra..253
74. Pickled pearl onions..256
75. Marinated peppers..259
76. Pickled bell peppers..263
77. Pickled hot peppers...266
78. Pickled jalapeño pepper rings................................270
79. Pickled yellow pepper rings....................................274

80. Pickled sweet green tomatoes..................................277
81. Pickled mixed vegetables.......................................280
82. Pickled bread-and-butter zucchini..........................283
83. Chayote and pear relish..286
84. Piccalilli..289
85. Pickle relish..292
86. Pickled corn relish..295
87. Pickled green tomato relish....................................298
88. Pickled horseradish sauce......................................301
89. Pickled pepper-onion relish....................................304
90. Spicy jicama relish...306
91. Tangy tomatillo relish..309
92. No sugar added pickled beets.................................312
93. Sweet pickle cucumber..315
94. Sliced dill pickles..318
95. Sliced sweet pickles...321
96. Lemon & Dill Kraut...324
97. Chinese Kimchi...326
98. Fermented Carrot Sticks..329
99. Carrots with an Indian Twist..................................332
100. Radish Bombs..335

CONCLUSION..338

INTRODUCTION

What is fermentation?

Fermentation is a wonderful way to naturally preserve food and great if you have a glut of homegrown produce and don't know what to do with it!!

A magical microbial transformation happens when veggies are fermented naturally, the vitamin C content shoots up markedly, beneficial bacteria are produced, gut healing compounds are formed and the immune system is given a tremendous boost!

So you essentially end up with superfoods that are nutritionally superior, pre-digested, vitamin enhanced and absolutely packed with gut healing probiotics!!

Fermentation is when microorganisms, such as bacteria and yeast, break down and transform a substance into acids or alcohol. As the breakdown occurs, carbon dioxide is released, which leads to that tell-tale frothing and bubbling that is a sure sign that fermentation is well on its way.

Is fermentation safe?

Fermentation may seem like a rather daunting task, but despite common fears and trepidations, fermentation is extremely safe. So long as you follow all the methods and tips found in this book, you are not likely to encounter anything scary or off-putting in the least.

The lactic acid bacteria that carries out the fermentation process is anaerobic, meaning it does not need oxygen to survive. As it transforms carbohydrates into acid, it actually kills off any harmful bacteria present, too. This includes mold, which is aerobic and cannot grow without oxygen.

The salt that you use in fermentation is also key in allowing the good bacteria to flourish and keeping the bad bacteria at bay. Salt plays a role in preserving nutrients and keeping the chiles crisp and fresh during fermentation.

Do you know what all this means? Lactic-acid fermentation is actually one of the safest ways of preparing and preserving food.

Ultimately, common sense and your five senses are the best tools you can use and will take you far on your fermentation journey. If something looks, smells, or tastes off, simply don't eat it.

All in all, the steps taken to produce fermented hot sauce counteract the production of bad bacteria and create the ideal conditions for probiotics to flourish and a healthy, delicious ferment to come to fruition.

Best Fermented Foods

A. **Cheese:** Cheese is one of the most commonly fermented dairy products. Many varieties of cheese are fermented, including cheddar and Parmesan. Fresh cheeses, such as cottage and mozzarella, are not.

B. **Chocolate:** The process by which most chocolate is made starts with the fermentation of the cacao beans. Fermentation breaks down the carbohydrates in the beans and develops that rich chocolate flavor you've come to know and love.

C. **Sourdough Bread:** Sourdough begins with the use of a "starter," which is simply a mix of flour and water that has fermented. When this starter is incorporated into bread dough, the natural yeasts help the bread rise and also impart the tangy flavor sourdough bread is famous for.

D. Buttermilk: Traditionally, buttermilk is made by fermenting the liquid left behind from churning butter. These days, buttermilk is more commonly made by adding lactic acid bacteria to regular milk to encourage the fermentation process.

E. Soy Sauce: This salty condiment is traditionally (and still commonly) made from a fermented soybean paste. Soy sauce has been around in one form or another for nearly 2,000 years.

F. Vinegar: This tangy, acidic condiment is —you guessed it—fermented! But just what is fermented to make vinegar? Anything from raisins and pomegranates to coconut water and barley can be fermented to produce vinegar.

G. Beer and Wine: These common alcoholic beverages are produced through the act of fermentation. Beer is the result of fermenting the starches in grains, whereas wine is produced by fermenting the sugars in grape juice.

FERMENTED SAUCES

1. Louisiana-style hot sauce

MAKES 16 OUNCES

Ingredients:

- 1 pound (about 10) fresh cayenne or tabasco peppers, stemmed
- 2 teaspoons non-iodized salt
- ½ cup white wine vinegar or white vinegar
- 2 garlic cloves

Directions:

a) In a blender or food processor, combine the chiles and salt. Blend until a mash forms and a brine releases from the chiles.
b) Pack the mash into a clean jar and press it down until the natural brine covers the chiles, leaving at least 1 inch of headspace.
c) Place a cartouche, if using, then screw the lid on tightly and store the jar at room temperature away from direct sunlight to ferment for 2 weeks. Burp the jar daily.
d) Once fermentation is complete, combine the mash (natural brine included), vinegar, and garlic in a food processor or blender. Blend until the sauce is as smooth as possible.
e) Store the hot sauce in an airtight container in the refrigerator for up to 1 year.

2. Chimichurri verde

MAKES 8 OUNCES

Ingredients:

- 2 cups freshly chopped parsley
- 1 cup freshly chopped cilantro
- 2 scallions, both white and green parts, chopped
- 4 garlic cloves, minced
- 1 fresh red chile (such as cayenne or tabasco), stemmed and chopped
- 1½ teaspoons non-iodized salt
- ¼ cup red wine vinegar
- ¼ cup olive oil, for serving

Directions:

a) In a mixing bowl, combine the parsley, cilantro, scallions, garlic, and red chile. Sprinkle with the salt. Using your hands, massage the salt into the veggies. Let it sit for 10 minutes to allow a brine to form.

a) Once the natural brine has been released, pack the mixture and brine into a clean jar. Press the mixture down until the brine covers the veggies.

b) Place a cartouche, if using, then screw the lid on tightly and store the jar at room temperature away from direct sunlight to ferment for 5 days. Burp the jar daily.

c) Once fermentation is complete, combine the ferment and red wine vinegar in a blender or food processor. Blend until well combined.

d) Store the chimichurri in the refrigerator for up to 3 months. When ready to serve, add 1 tablespoon of olive oil per $\frac{1}{4}$ cup of chimichurri.

3. Ají amarillo sauce

MAKES 16 OUNCES

Ingredients:

For the paste

- 4 ounces (about 15) dried ají amarillo peppers, stemmed and torn into pieces
- 6 garlic cloves
- 3 scallions, both white and green parts, sliced
- 2½ cups non-chlorinated water
- 2 tablespoons non-iodized salt
- 5 tablespoons lime juice
- 2 tablespoons reserved brine

For the sauce

- 2 cups ají amarillo paste
- 1 cup evaporated milk
- 1 cup queso fresco or feta cheese
- ¼ cup crushed crackers or bread crumbs

Directions:

a) To make the paste: In a clean jar, combine the chiles, garlic, and scallions.
b) In a separate vessel, make a brine by combining the water and salt.
c) Place a weight, if using, then pour the brine into the jar, leaving at least 1 inch of headspace. Screw the lid on tightly and store the jar at room temperature away from direct sunlight to ferment for 10 days. Burp the jar daily.
d) Once fermentation is complete, strain the ferment, reserving 2 tablespoons of the brine.
e) In a blender or food processor, combine the ferment, lime juice, and reserved brine. Blend until smooth.
f) Store the paste in the fridge for up to 6 months.
g) To make the sauce: In a blender or food processor, combine the ají amarillo paste, evaporated milk, cheese, and crackers or bread crumbs.
h) Blend until smooth.

4. Garlicky green chili sauce

MAKES 16 OUNCES

Ingredients:

- 1 pound (about 6) fresh Hatch chiles, stemmed
- 8 garlic cloves
- 2 teaspoons non-iodized salt
- 2 teaspoons cumin seeds
- 1 teaspoon ground oregano
- $\frac{1}{4}$ cup white vinegar
- 1 tablespoon granulated sugar

Directions:

a) In a blender or food processor, combine the chiles, garlic, salt, cumin seeds, and oregano. Blend until roughly chopped and a natural brine has been released. Pour the mixture into a clean jar.

b) Place a cartouche, if using, then screw the lid on tightly and store the jar at room temperature away from direct sunlight to ferment for 5 days. Burp the jar daily.

c) Once fermentation is complete, combine the ferment, vinegar, and sugar in a food processor or blender. Blend until smooth.

d) Store the sauce in the refrigerator for up to 1 year.

5. Chipotle hot sauce

MAKES 16 OUNCES

Ingredients:

- 2 ounces (about 15) dried chipotle peppers, stemmed
- 6 garlic cloves
- ½ white or yellow onion, halved
- 2 cups non-chlorinated water
- 1 tablespoon plus 1 teaspoon non-iodized salt
- ½ cup orange juice
- ½ cup apple cider vinegar
- ¼ cup reserved brine
- 2 tablespoons tomato paste
- 1 tablespoon granulated sugar
- 1 teaspoon cumin seeds

Directions:

a) In a clean jar, combine the chiles, garlic, and onion.
b) In a separate vessel, make a brine by combining the water and salt.
c) Place a weight, if using, then pour the brine into the jar, leaving at least 1 inch of headspace. Screw the lid on tightly and store the jar at room temperature away from direct sunlight to ferment for 1 week. Burp the jar daily.
d) Once fermentation is complete, strain the ferment, reserving $\frac{1}{4}$ cup of the brine.
e) In a blender or food processor, combine the ferment, orange juice, vinegar, reserved brine, tomato paste, sugar, and cumin seeds. Blend until smooth.
f) Keep the sauce stored in the refrigerator for up to 1 year.

6. Ají picante

MAKES 16 OUNCES

Ingredients:

- 1 ounce (about 4) fresh ají chirca or habanero peppers, stemmed and chopped
- 6 scallions, both white and green parts, chopped
- 1 cup freshly chopped cilantro
- 2 medium tomatoes, chopped
- 1 tablespoon non-iodized salt
- 1 cup water
- ¼ cup reserved brine
- ¼ cup white vinegar
- 2 tablespoons lime juice
- 2 teaspoons granulated sugar
- ¼ cup avocado or sunflower oil, for serving

Directions:

a) In a mixing bowl, combine the chiles, scallions, cilantro, and tomatoes. Sprinkle the vegetables with the salt.

b) Using your hands, massage the salt into the veggies until a brine begins to form. Let the veggies sit for 30 minutes, or until enough brine has formed to cover the ingredients in a jar.

c) Pack the mash into a clean jar, pressing it down to ensure the brine covers the mash.

d) Place a cartouche, if using, then screw the lid on tightly and store the jar at room temperature to ferment for 5 days. Burp the jar daily.

e) Once fermentation is complete, strain the mash, reserving $\frac{1}{4}$ cup of the brine.

f) Combine the mash, water, reserved brine, vinegar, lime juice, and sugar in a food processor or blender. Pulse lightly until combined well but not pureed completely. For a slightly chunkier version, you can skip the pulsing step and simply mix the ingredients by hand.

g) Keep the ají picante stored in an airtight container in the refrigerator for up to 1 year.

h) Mix in 1 tablespoon of oil per 1 cup of sauce right before serving.

7. Hawaiian chile water

MAKES 12 OUNCES

- 1½ ounces (about 6) fresh Hawaiian peppers or habanero peppers, stemmed and sliced into strips
- 1 (1-inch) piece fresh ginger, sliced
- 2 garlic cloves, crushed
- 2½ cups non-chlorinated water
- 2 tablespoons alaea salt (traditional) or non-iodized salt
- ½ cup white vinegar
- ½ cup reserved brine

Directions:

a) In a clean jar, combine the chiles, ginger, and garlic.
b) In a separate vessel, make a brine by combining the water and salt.
c) Place a weight, if using, then pour the brine into the jar, leaving at least 1 inch of headspace. Screw the lid on tightly and store the jar at room temperature away from direct sunlight to ferment for 1 week. Burp the jar daily.
d) Once fermentation is complete, strain the ferment, reserving $\frac{1}{2}$ cup of the brine.
e) Place the ferment, vinegar, and reserved brine in a food processor or blender. Pulse until the ingredients are finely chopped.
f) Store the chile water in the refrigerator for up to 1 year.

FERMENTED DAIRY

8. Traditional Vegan Yogurt

Makes about 2 to 2½ cups

Ingredients:

- 2 cups raw, unsalted cashews
- 3 cups filtered water
- 1 teaspoon pure maple syrup or agave nectar
- 2 probiotic capsules or ½ teaspoon probiotic powder

Directions:

a) Blend the cashews, water, and syrup or nectar until smooth. Pour into a medium saucepan, and heat over low heat until warm but not hot.

b) Once it is lukewarm, pour the cashew milk into a clean, nonmetallic container such as a glass bowl or ceramic crock.

c) Add the contents of the probiotic capsules (discarding the empty capsule shells) or probiotic powder to the cashew milk. Stir the ingredients together until combined.

d) Cover the container, and let it sit undisturbed in a warm setting for eight to ten hours, or more if you prefer a tangier yogurt.

e) Scoop out the thickened yogurt, and reserve the whey for another use.

9. Cultured Coconut Cream

Makes about 1 cup

Ingredients:

- One 14-ounce can coconut milk (regular coconut milk, not the "light" or low-fat versions)

- 1 probiotic capsule or $\frac{1}{4}$ teaspoon probiotic powder

Directions:

a) In a small glass or ceramic bowl with a lid, empty the can of coconut milk. (Do not use a metal bowl, as metal can inhibit the culturing process.) If the cream and water have separated, mix them together.

b) Stir in the contents of the probiotic capsule (discarding the empty capsule shell) or the probiotic powder.

c) Cover the bowl with a clean cloth, and leave in an undisturbed, warm setting for eight to ten hours. Remove the cloth, cover the bowl with a lid, and refrigerate.

d) After the mixture has cooled for at least an hour, the coconut cream is ready for use. The mixture will have separated during the culturing/cooling process, and the coconut cream is the thick top layer.

e) Scoop out the cream, and either use it immediately or transfer it to another lidded glass container and store it in the refrigerator until you're ready to use it.

f) The thinner liquid below the cream can be saved and added to smoothies and juices or used as a "starter" to culture other foods. The cream and starter liquid will last for about one week in the fridge.

10. Homemade Fermented Yogurt

Makes about 1 quart/liter

Ingredients:

- 3 cups raw, unsalted cashews
- 2 cups filtered water
- 1 probiotic capsule or $\frac{1}{4}$ teaspoon probiotic powder
- Pomegranate arils (seeds) or pitted frozen or fresh cherries for garnish (optional)

Directions:

a) In a medium glass or ceramic bowl with a lid, combine the cashews with the water, and pour in the contents of the probiotic capsule (discarding the empty capsule shell) or the probiotic powder. Stir the ingredients together until combined.

b) Attach the lid, and let sit for eight to twenty-four hours, depending on how tangy you like your yogurt.

c) Puree the ingredients in a blender until smooth, then return the yogurt to the bowl. Garnish with pomegranate arils or cherries if desired, and enjoy immediately, or refrigerate for up to four days.

11. Dairy-Free Cream

Makes about 1½ cups

Ingredients:

- ½ cup almond milk
- 1 cup raw, unsalted cashews
- 2 fresh Medjool dates, pitted and coarsely chopped
- 2 probiotic capsules or ½ teaspoon probiotic powder

Directions:

a) In a glass or ceramic bowl with a lid, combine the almond milk, cashews, and date pieces. Add the contents of the probiotic capsule (discarding the empty capsule shell) or the probiotic powder, and stir into the cashew mixture.

b) Cover the bowl, and let it sit in a warm, undisturbed setting for eight to ten hours or until you achieve your desired tanginess.

c) Blend the ingredients together until they are smooth, adding a small amount of water as necessary to enable blending. Serve immediately or refrigerate for up to one week.

12. Gluten-Free, Dairy-Free Rejuvelac

Makes 3 cups

Ingredients:

- ½ cup whole buckwheat grains (or other whole grains of your choice)
- 3 cups filtered water

Directions:

a) Place the grains in a 1-quart glass jar, and add just enough water to cover. Place a double layer of cheesecloth over the mouth of the jar, and secure it in place with a rubber band. Allow the grains to soak for eight hours or overnight; drain, discarding the liquid.

b) Add 3 cups of filtered water, cover with a fresh cheesecloth, and secure it with a rubber band. Put the jar in a warm place but out of direct sunlight for one to three days. The water will turn whitish-colored and cloudy and will develop a slightly tart flavor.

c) Strain off the grains; these can be reused to make a second batch of rejuvelac if you like. Cover the liquid with a lid, and store in the fridge for up to two weeks.

13. Yogurt Cheese

Makes about 1 quart/liter

Ingredients:

- 3 cups raw, unsalted cashews
- 2 cups filtered water
- 1 probiotic capsule or ¼ teaspoon probiotic powder

Directions:

a) In a medium glass or ceramic bowl with a lid, combine the cashews and water, and add the contents of the probiotic capsule, discarding the empty capsule shell, or the probiotic powder; stir together until combined. Cover and let sit for eight to twenty-four hours, depending on how tangy you like your yogurt cheese.

b) Puree the ingredients in a blender until smooth. Place a cheesecloth-lined sieve over a deep bowl to allow the excess water to drip out of the yogurt.

c) Pour the yogurt into the cheesecloth-lined sieve, and allow it to sit for a few hours until it reaches your desired thickness. You may need to gently squeeze out the excess moisture to ensure the yogurt thickens sufficiently.

d) Place the yogurt cheese into a cheesecloth-lined mold of your choice, and refrigerate for four to six hours or until firm. You can pull the edges of the cheesecloth over the top if you prefer, but it isn't necessary. Remove the cheese from the mold, then peel away the cheesecloth. Serve.

e) Keeps in the refrigerator in a covered container for up to one week.

14. Almond Farmer's Cheese

Makes 1 small block

Ingredients:

- 1 quart/liter unsweetened almond milk
- 1 tablespoon store-bought or homemade apple cider vinegar
- Fresh herbs, minced
- 1 teaspoon unrefined sea salt

Directions:

a) In a medium pot, heat the milk over low heat, stirring occasionally to prevent scalding or sticking. When it looks like the almond milk is just about to boil, remove from the heat; if you prefer to use a candy or canning thermometer (it's not necessary), remove the pot from the stove when the milk reaches 180 to 190°F.

b) Add the vinegar, stir gently for a few seconds, and then leave it undisturbed for a few minutes.

c) While the vinegar is working, line a colander with cheesecloth. Once the curds and whey have separated, pour them through it over a sink if you want to discard the whey or over a large bowl if you prefer to keep the whey for later use.

d) Fold the excess cheesecloth over the curds, and place a clean weight on top; allow it to sit for one to two hours to press out any remaining whey. Alternatively, simply tie up the corners of the cheesecloth, and allow the curds to sit for one to two hours to continue draining.

e) If using herbs, add them to the cheese after straining and prior to setting up the cheese in a mold (see next step). Alternatively, you can line the bottom of the mold with your desired herbs.

f) Stir in the salt until it is well combined with the cheese, and place the cheese in a mold or small glass or ceramic bowl and allow to set in the fridge for four to six hours.

g) Serve immediately or store in a covered dish in the refrigerator for up to one week.

15. Walnut Thyme Cheese

Makes 1 small block

Ingredients:

- 1 cup raw, unsalted walnuts
- ¼ cup filtered water
- 2 capsules probiotics or ½ teaspoon probiotic powder
- 1 teaspoon extra-virgin olive oil
- Three 2-inch sprigs fresh thyme, plus a few more for garnish (optional)
- 1 teaspoon unrefined sea salt
- ½ cup coconut oil

Directions:

a) In a small glass or ceramic bowl, combine the walnuts and water. Empty the contents of the probiotic capsules or the probiotic powder into the bowl, and stir to combine.

b) Cover and let sit in a warm, undisturbed spot for two days.

c) In a small frying pan over low to medium heat, sauté the olive oil and thyme until the sprigs are lightly crisped (about 3 to 5 minutes). Remove from the heat. Once cool, pull the thyme leaves off the sprigs, and sprinkle them across the base of a small glass dish.

d) Pour the walnut mixture into a blender, add the salt and coconut oil, and blend until it is completely smooth; pour it into the glass dish coated in thyme leaves. Refrigerate, uncovered, until it is set

e) Gently remove the cheese from the glass bowl, and serve upside down so the thyme leaves are on the top of the cheese. Garnish with thyme sprigs if desired. It keeps in the refrigerator, covered, for about one month.

16.   Bracotta Cheese

Makes about 3 cups or 1 medium-size block

Ingredients:

- 1 cup raw, unsalted Brazil nuts
- 1 cup raw, unsalted cashews
- 1 cup filtered water
- 2 probiotic capsules or ½ teaspoon probiotic powder
- ⅓ cup coconut oil
- 1 teaspoon unrefined sea salt
- 1 tablespoon filtered water

Directions:

a) In a small to medium bowl with a lid, combine the Brazil nuts, cashews, and the cup of water. Empty the contents of the probiotic supplements (discarding the empty capsule shells) or probiotic powder into the bowl, and mix together.

b) Allow the mixture to culture for twenty-four to forty-eight hours; the longer fermentation time will develop a stronger flavor for the cheese.

c) Pour the Brazil nut–cashew mixture into a blender. Add the oil, salt, and 1 tablespoon water, and blend until smooth; this may require effort and a longer blending time to ensure a consistently smooth texture.

d) Pour the mixture into a cheesecloth-lined mold of your choice. Cover and refrigerate until it is set (at least two to four hours).

e) Remove the cheese from the mold, and unwrap from the cheesecloth. Serve. Refrigerate in a covered container for up to three weeks.

17. Macadamia Cream Cheese

Makes 1 small block

Ingredients:

- ½ cup raw, unsalted macadamia nuts
- ½ cup raw, unsalted cashews
- ½ cup filtered water, plus 3 tablespoons
- 1 probiotic capsule or ¼ teaspoon probiotic powder
- 3 fresh Medjool dates, pitted
- ⅓ cup coconut oil
- ¼ teaspoon unrefined sea salt

Directions:

a) In a glass or ceramic bowl, combine the macadamia nuts, cashews, ½ cup water, and the probiotic capsule (discarding the empty capsule shell) or probiotic powder; stir until mixed, and cover. In a separate bowl mix the dates with the remaining 3 tablespoons of water, and cover. Allow both to sit overnight for twelve hours.

b) In a blender combine both mixtures, add the salt, and blend until smooth. Add the coconut oil and continue blending. You may need to push the ingredients down with a spatula a few times to ensure a creamy, smooth consistency. Pour into a cheesecloth-lined dish or mold.

c) Refrigerate for one to two hours, or until it is set. Serve. Store in the refrigerator, covered, for up to one month.

18.   Aged Smoked Cheese

Makes 1 medium-size block

Ingredients:

- 2 cups raw, unsalted cashews
- 1 cup filtered water
- 2 probiotic capsules or $\frac{1}{2}$ teaspoon probiotic powder
- $\frac{1}{2}$ cup coconut oil
- 4 teaspoons smoked unrefined sea salt, divided

Directions:

a) In a glass or ceramic bowl with a lid, combine the cashews and water, and empty the probiotic capsules (discarding the empty capsule shells) or probiotic powder into the cashew-water mixture, and stir until combined. Cover and let sit for twenty-four hours.

b) Pour the cultured cashews and their liquid into a blender. Add the oil and 2 teaspoons of the salt, and blend until smooth. You may need to push the ingredients down with a spatula a few times to ensure a creamy, smooth consistency.

c) Pour the cheese mixture into a cheesecloth-lined bowl that is the shape you'd like the finished cheese to be. Refrigerate for four to six hours, or until it is firm. Remove the cheese from the bowl, and peel away the cheesecloth.

d) Gently rub the remaining 2 teaspoons of salt over the full surface of the cheese, including the bottom. Carefully place the cheese on a wire rack in a cool, dark, and undisturbed place, and allow the cheese to air-dry for seven to twenty-eight days, or longer if desired.

e) After you have aged the cheese, refrigerate and serve, or store in a covered container in the refrigerator for up to one month.

19. Aged Miso Cheese

Makes 1 medium-size block

Ingredients:

- 2 cups raw, unsalted cashews
- 1 cup filtered water
- 1 tablespoon dark miso
- 3 teaspoons unrefined sea salt, divided
- $\frac{1}{2}$ cup coconut oil

Directions:

a) In a glass or ceramic bowl with a lid, combine the cashews, water, and miso, and stir until they are combined. Cover and let sit for twenty-four hours.

b) Pour the cultured cashews into a blender. Add 1 teaspoon of the salt as well as the oil, and blend until smooth. You may need to push the ingredients down with a spatula a few times to ensure a creamy, smooth consistency.

c) Pour the cheese mixture into a cheesecloth-lined bowl that is the shape you'd like the finished cheese to be. Refrigerate for four to six hours, or until it is firm. Remove the cheese from the bowl, and peel away the cheesecloth.

d) Gently rub the remaining 2 teaspoons of salt over the full surface of the cheese, including the bottom. Carefully place it on a wire rack in a cool, dark, and undisturbed place, and allow the cheese to air-dry for seven to twenty-eight days, or longer if desired.

e) After you have aged the cheese, refrigerate and serve, or store in a covered container in the refrigerator for up to one month.

20.   Aged Savorella Cheese

Makes 1 medium-size block

Ingredients:

- 2 cups raw, unsalted cashews
- ⅔ cup filtered water
- ⅓ cup sauerkraut brine
- 3 teaspoons unrefined sea salt, divided
- ½ cup coconut oil

Directions:

a) In a glass or ceramic bowl with a lid, combine the cashews, water, and brine, and stir well. Cover and let sit for twenty-four hours.

b) Pour the cultured cashews and their liquid into a blender. Add 1 teaspoon of the salt as well as the oil, and blend until smooth. You may need to push the ingredients down with a spatula a few times to ensure a creamy, smooth consistency.

c) Pour the cheese mixture into a cheesecloth-lined bowl that is the shape you'd like the finished cheese to be. Refrigerate for four to six hours, or until it is firm. Remove from the bowl, and peel away the cheesecloth.

d) Gently rub the remaining 2 teaspoons of salt over the full surface of the cheese, including the bottom. Carefully place it on a wire rack in a cool, dark, and undisturbed place, and allow the cheese to air-dry for two weeks.

e) After you have aged the cheese, refrigerate and serve, or store in a covered container in the refrigerator for up to one month.

SAUERKRAUT & PICKLES

21.   Basic Sauerkraut

Makes approximately 3 to 4 quarts

Ingredients:

- 2 small to medium heads green cabbage, shredded
- 1 tablespoon juniper berries, coarsely cracked
- 3 tablespoons unrefined fine sea salt
- 1 quart (or liter) filtered water

Directions:

a) Place the green cabbage in a large, clean crock or a large glass or ceramic bowl; push it down with your clean fist or a wooden spoon to release the juices. Add a pinch of the juniper berries throughout the process of adding cabbage.

b) In a pitcher or a large measuring cup, dissolve the salt in the water, stirring if necessary to encourage the salt to dissolve. Pour the saltwater over the cabbage until it is submerged, leaving a couple of inches of room at the top for the cabbage to expand.

c) Place a plate that fits inside the crock or bowl over the cabbage-water mixture, and weigh it down with food-safe weights or a bowl or jar of water, making sure the vegetables remain submerged under the brine as they ferment.

d) Cover with a lid or a cloth, and allow it to ferment for at least two weeks, checking periodically to ensure that the cabbage mixture is still submerged below the water line.

e) After two weeks the sauerkraut will still be fairly crunchy; if you like a more traditional sauerkraut, allow it to ferment longer to soften the cabbage further.

f) If any mold forms on the surface of the crock, simply scoop it out. It will not spoil the sauerkraut unless it gets deeper inside the crock. It may form where the mixture meets the air, but it rarely forms deeper inside the crock.

g) After two weeks, or longer if you prefer, dish out the sauerkraut into jars or a bowl, cover, and place in the fridge, where it will last for at least a few months to a year.

22. Spiced Sauerkraut

Makes approximately 2 quarts

Ingredients:

- 1 large or 2 small heads green cabbage, shredded
- 6 dried or fresh whole cayenne chiles (or more for a hotter sauerkraut)
- 3 garlic cloves, minced
- 4 tablespoons unrefined fine sea salt or 8 tablespoons unrefined coarse sea salt
- 1 quart (or liter) filtered water

Directions:

a) In a large, clean crock or a large glass or ceramic bowl, layer the green cabbage, chiles, and garlic until the crock is full or you have used all the ingredients.

b) Using a wooden spoon or your clean fist, push down the cabbage mixture to make it more compact and to release the juices.

c) In a pitcher or large measuring cup, dissolve the salt in the water, stirring if necessary to encourage the salt to dissolve. Pour the saltwater over the cabbage mixture until the ingredients are submerged, leaving a couple of inches of room at the top for the ingredients to expand.

d) Place a plate that fits inside the crock or bowl over the cabbage-water mixture, and weigh it down with food-safe weights or a bowl or jar of water, making sure the vegetables remain submerged under the water-salt brine as they ferment.

e) Cover with a lid or cloth, and allow it to ferment for at least two weeks, checking periodically to ensure that the cabbage mixture is still submerged below the water line.

f) If any mold forms on the surface, simply scoop it out. It will not spoil the sauerkraut unless it gets deeper inside the crock. It may form where the mixture meets the air, but it rarely forms deeper inside the crock.

g) After two weeks, or longer if you prefer a tangier sauerkraut, dish out the sauerkraut into jars or a bowl, cover, and place in the fridge, where it will usually last for at least a year. Serve topped with slices of the chiles, if desired.

23. Five-Minute Broccoli Sauerkraut

Makes approximately 1 quart

Ingredients:

- 1 (10-ounce or 282-mg) package broccoli coleslaw mix
- 1 red bell pepper, cored and julienned
- 1 jalapeño pepper, cored and julienned
- 3 tablespoons unrefined fine sea salt or 6 tablespoons unrefined coarse sea salt
- 1 quart (or liter) filtered water

Directions:

a) In a large, clean crock or large glass or ceramic bowl, alternate layers of broccoli slaw, bell pepper, and jalapeño pepper inside the crock until the mixture is approximately 1 to 2 inches from the top of the crock or bowl or until you have used all the ingredients.

b) Push the vegetables down with your clean fist or a wooden spoon to release the juices as you go.

c) In a pitcher or large measuring cup, dissolve the salt in the water, stirring if necessary to encourage the salt to dissolve. Pour the saltwater over the vegetable mixture until the ingredients are submerged, leaving a couple of inches of room at the top for the vegetables to expand.

d) Place a plate that fits inside the crock or bowl over the vegetable-water mixture, and weigh it down with food-safe weights or a bowl or jar of water, making sure the vegetables remain submerged under the brine as they ferment.

e) Cover with a lid or a cloth, and allow it to ferment for at least two weeks, checking periodically to ensure that the cabbage mixture is still submerged below the water line. After two weeks the sauerkraut will still be fairly crunchy; if you like a more traditional sauerkraut, allow it to ferment longer to soften the cabbage further.

f) If any mold forms on the surface, simply scoop it out. It will not spoil the sauerkraut unless it gets deeper inside the crock. It may form where the mixture meets the air, but it rarely forms deeper inside the crock.

g) After one week, or longer if you prefer a tarter-tasting sauerkraut, dish out the sauerkraut into jars or a bowl, cover, and place in the fridge, where it will last for at least a few months to a year.

24. Pineapple Sauerkraut

Makes about 3 quarts

Ingredients:

- 1 medium pineapple, top, core, and skin removed, julienned
- 1 medium head cabbage, thinly grated
- 2 medium carrots, grated
- ¼ small onion, grated
- 3 tablespoons unrefined fine sea salt or 6 tablespoons unrefined coarse sea salt
- 2 quarts (or liters) filtered water
- Cilantro sprigs for garnish (optional)

Directions:

a) In a large, clean 4-quart crock or a large glass or ceramic bowl, alternate layers of pineapple, cabbage, carrots, and onion until the mixture is approximately 1 to 2 inches from the top of the crock or bowl or until you have used all the ingredients. Push down the vegetables with your clean fist or a wooden spoon to release the juices as you go.

b) In a pitcher or large measuring cup, dissolve the salt in the water, stirring if necessary to encourage the salt to dissolve. Pour the saltwater over the pineapple mixture until the ingredients are submerged, leaving a couple of inches of room at the top for the ingredients to expand.

c) Place a plate that fits inside the crock or bowl over the pineapple-water mixture, and weigh it down with food-safe weights or a bowl or jar of water, making sure the fruit and vegetables remain submerged under the brine as they ferment.

d) Cover with a lid or a cloth, and allow it to ferment for at least two weeks, checking periodically to ensure that the pineapple mixture is still submerged below the water line.

e) After two weeks the sauerkraut will still be fairly crunchy; if you like a more traditional sauerkraut, allow it to ferment longer to soften the cabbage further.

f) If any mold forms on the surface, simply scoop it out. It will not spoil the sauerkraut unless it gets deeper inside the crock. It may form where the mixture meets the air, but it rarely forms deeper inside the crock.

g) After two weeks, or longer if you prefer a tangier sauerkraut, dish out the sauerkraut into jars or a bowl, cover, and place in the fridge, where it will last for at least a few months to a year. Serve topped with cilantro sprigs, if desired.

25. Purple Sauerkraut

Makes approximate 2 to 2½ quarts

Ingredients:

- 1 small head green cabbage, shredded
- 1 small head purple cabbage, shredded
- 2 apples, thinly sliced
- 3 tablespoons unrefined fine sea salt or 6 tablespoons unrefined coarse sea salt
- 1 quart (or liter) filtered water

Directions:

a) In a large, clean crock or a large glass or ceramic bowl, layer the green cabbage, purple cabbage, and apples until the mixture is approximately 1 to 2 inches from the top of the crock or bowl or you have used all the ingredients.

b) Push down the cabbage and apple mixture with your clean fist or a wooden spoon to make it more compact and to release the juices as you go.

c) In a pitcher or large measuring cup, dissolve the salt in the water, stirring if necessary to encourage the salt to dissolve. Pour the saltwater over the cabbage-apple mixture until the ingredients are submerged, leaving a couple of inches of room at the top for the ingredients to expand.

d) Place a plate that fits inside the crock or bowl over the cabbage-apple-water mixture, and weigh it down with food-safe weights or a bowl or jar of water, making sure the vegetables remain submerged under the brine as they ferment.

e) Cover with a lid or a cloth, and allow it to ferment for at least two weeks, checking periodically to ensure that the cabbage-apple mixture is still submerged below the water line. After two weeks the sauerkraut will still be fairly crunchy; if you like a more traditional sauerkraut, allow it to ferment longer to soften the cabbage further.

f) If any mold forms on the surface, simply scoop it out. It will not spoil the sauerkraut unless it gets deeper inside the crock. It may form where the mixture meets the air, but it rarely forms deeper inside the crock.

g) After two weeks, or longer if you prefer a tangier sauerkraut, dish out the sauerkraut into jars or a bowl, cover, and place in the fridge, where it will usually last for at least a year.

26. Spicy Dill Fermented Pickles

Makes about 2 quarts

Ingredients:

- 4 large or 6 medium cucumbers or lemon cucumbers, quartered lengthwise
- 3 dried cayenne chili peppers
- 2 garlic cloves
- 4 sprigs fresh dill
- 3 tablespoons unrefined fine sea salt or 6 tablespoons unrefined coarse sea salt
- $1\frac{1}{2}$ quarts (or liters) or 6 cups filtered water

Directions:

a) In a large, clean crock or a large glass or ceramic bowl, combine the cucumbers, chili peppers, garlic, and dill.

b) In a pitcher or large measuring cup, dissolve the salt in the water, stirring if necessary to encourage the salt to dissolve. Pour the saltwater over the cucumber mixture until the ingredients are submerged, leaving a couple of inches of room at the top for the ingredients to expand.

c) Place a plate that fits inside the crock or bowl over the cucumber-water mixture, and weigh it down with food-safe weights or a bowl or jar of water, making sure the vegetables remain submerged under the brine as they ferment.

d) Cover with a lid or a cloth, and allow it to ferment for five to seven days, or longer if you prefer a tangier taste; check the mixture periodically to ensure that it is still submerged below the water line.

e) If any mold forms on the surface, simply scoop it out. It will not spoil the pickles unless it gets deeper inside the crock. It may form where the mixture meets the air, but it rarely forms deeper inside the crock.

f) After one week, or longer if you prefer a tangier pickle, dish out the pickles into jars or a bowl, cover, and place in the fridge, where they will usually last for up to a year.

27. Salvadoran Salsa

Makes about 1 quart/liter

Ingredients:

- ½ green cabbage
- 1 to 2 carrots
- 1 green apple, cored and quartered
- One 2-inch piece fresh ginger
- ½ cayenne chili
- ½ small purple onion
- One 2-inch piece fresh turmeric
- 3 tablespoons unrefined fine sea salt or 6 tablespoons unrefined coarse sea salt
- 1 quart (or liter) filtered water

Directions:

a) Using a food processor with a coarse grating blade, shred the cabbage, carrots, apple, ginger, chili, onion, and turmeric.

b) Transfer to a crock or a large glass or ceramic bowl, and mix them together well.

c) In a pitcher or large measuring cup, dissolve the salt in the water, stirring if necessary to encourage the salt to dissolve. Pour the saltwater over the salsa mixture until the ingredients are submerged, leaving a couple of inches of room at the top for the ingredients to expand.

d) Place a plate that fits inside the crock or bowl over the salsa-water mixture, and weigh it down with food-safe weights or a bowl or jar of water, making sure the vegetables remain submerged under the brine as they ferment.

e) Cover with a lid or a cloth, and allow it to ferment for five to seven days, checking periodically to ensure that the salsa mixture is still submerged below the water line.

f) After one week, dish out the salsa into jars or a bowl, cover, and place in the fridge, where it will usually last up to one year.

28. Star Anise Carrots

Makes about 1 quart/liter

Ingredients:

- 1½ pounds carrots, grated
- 3 whole star anise pods
- 3 tablespoons unrefined fine sea salt or 6 tablespoons unrefined coarse sea salt
- 1 quart (or liter) filtered water

Directions:

a) In a medium, clean crock or a medium glass or ceramic bowl, combine the carrots and star anise.

b) In a pitcher or large measuring cup, dissolve the salt in the water, stirring if necessary to encourage the salt to dissolve.

c) Pour the saltwater over the carrot mixture until the ingredients are submerged, leaving a couple of inches of room at the top for the ingredients to expand.

d) Place a plate that fits inside the crock or bowl over the carrot-water mixture, and weigh it down with food-safe weights or a bowl or jar of water, making sure the carrots remain submerged under the brine as they ferment.

e) Cover with a lid or a cloth, and allow it to ferment for seven days, checking periodically to ensure that the carrot mixture is still submerged below the water line.

f) If any mold forms on the surface, simply scoop it out. It will not spoil the carrots unless it gets deeper inside the crock. It may form where the mixture meets the air, but it rarely forms deeper inside the crock.

g) After one week, dish out the carrots into jars or a bowl, cover, and place in the fridge, where it will usually last up to one year.

29. Cultured Onions

Makes about 2 cups

Ingredients:

- 2 small onions or 1 large onion, chopped into thin slices
- 1 tablespoon plus 1 teaspoon unrefined fine sea salt
- 1 cup filtered water

Directions:

a) Place the onions in a small sealable jar. In a measuring cup, dissolve the salt in the water, stirring if necessary to encourage the salt to dissolve.

b) Pour the saltwater over the onions in the jar until the ingredients are submerged, leaving some room at the top for the onions to expand.

c) Weigh down with a small ramekin, food-safe weight, or fermentation weights.

d) Cover with a lid or a cloth, and allow it to ferment for two to seven days. Shorter fermentation times result in stronger onions, and longer fermentation times mellow out the onion taste and increase the probiotic content.

e) After your desired fermentation time, remove the weights, seal, and store in the refrigerator, where the onions will usually last up to a year.

30. Red-Hot Hot Sauce

Makes about 2 to 3 cups

Ingredients:

- 1 pound red chiles
- 4 tablespoons unrefined fine sea salt or 8 tablespoons unrefined coarse sea salt
- 5 cups filtered water

Directions:

a) Wash the chiles and place them in a glass or ceramic jar with a wide opening or in a bowl.

b) In a pitcher or large measuring cup, dissolve the salt in the water, stirring if necessary to encourage the salt to dissolve. Pour the saltwater over the chiles until they are submerged, leaving a couple of inches of room at the top for the ingredients to expand.

c) Place a plate that fits inside the jar or bowl over the chili-water mixture, and weigh it down with food-safe weights or a small bowl or jar of water, making sure the chiles remain submerged under the brine as they ferment.

d) Cover with a lid or a cloth, and allow it to ferment for seven days, checking periodically to ensure that the chiles are still submerged below the water line. Strain off the brine, reserving it to add, as needed, to the chiles to obtain your desired hot-sauce consistency.

e) Place the chiles in a blender, and blend with enough brine to get a slightly thinner hot sauce than you would like; it will thicken as it sits. Pour into a jar or bowl, cover, and refrigerate, where it should last about one month.

31. Fermented Chopped Salad

Makes about 6 cups

Ingredients:

- 1 radish, finely chopped
- ½ small onion, finely chopped
- 1 turnip, chopped in ½-inch chunks
- 1 carrot, chopped in ½-inch chunks
- 3 small apples, chopped in ½-inch chunks
- Handful of green beans, chopped in 1-inch lengths
- 1 rutabaga, chopped in ½-inch chunks
- 1 to 2 grape leaves, kale leaves, or other large leafy greens (optional)
- 3 tablespoons unrefined fine sea salt or 6 tablespoons unrefined coarse sea salt
- 1 quart (or liter) filtered water

Directions:

a) In a medium bowl, toss together the radish, onion, turnip, carrot, apples, green beans, and rutabaga; transfer to a small crock. Place the grape leaves or other leafy greens over the top of the chopped salad ingredients to help hold them under the brine, and weigh down with food-safe weights or a jar or bowl of water.

b) In a pitcher or large measuring cup, dissolve the salt in the water, stirring if necessary to encourage the salt to dissolve. Pour the brine over the salad, cover with a lid or cloth, and allow it to ferment for one week.

c) Remove the weights, and remove and discard the grape leaves or other leafy greens. Dish out to jars or a bowl, cover, and refrigerate, where the salad should last six months to one year.

32.   Dill Cucumber Pickle Bites

Makes about 4 cups

Ingredients:

- 1 large cucumber, or 2-3 lemon cucumbers, chopped into 1-inch to 2-inch chunks
- 2 to 3 medium sprigs fresh dill
- 3 tablespoons unrefined fine sea salt or 6 tablespoons unrefined coarse sea salt
- 1 quart (or liter) filtered water

Directions:

a) Place the cucumbers in a large mason jar, interspersing dill sprigs throughout as you go. Weigh down the cucumbers with a food-safe clean weight inside the mason jar.

b) In a pitcher or large measuring cup, dissolve the salt in the water, stirring if necessary to encourage the salt to dissolve.

c) Pour the saltwater over the cucumbers until they are submerged, leaving some room at the top for the ingredients to expand.

d) Cover with a lid, and allow it to ferment for five to seven days, or until the cucumbers have reached your desired tanginess.

e) Remove the weights, replace the cover, and refrigerate, where the pickles will last for six months to one year.

33.   Zucchini Pickles

Makes about 8 cups

Ingredients:

- ½ teaspoon whole coriander seeds
- ½ dried cayenne chili, crushed
- 2 whole cloves
- ½ teaspoon anise seeds
- ½ teaspoon mustard seeds
- ½ teaspoon ground turmeric
- ¼ teaspoon ground pepper
- 2 large or 4 small zucchinis, cut into 1-inch chunks or long, thin spears, approximately 3 inches long, ½ inch across
- 3 tablespoons unrefined fine sea salt or 6 tablespoons unrefined coarse sea salt
- 2 quarts (or liters) filtered water

Directions:

a) Combine the coriander, chili, cloves, anise, mustard, turmeric, and pepper in a small to medium crock. Add the zucchini and stir to combine. Weigh down the zucchini with clean, food-safe weights or a jar or bowl of water.

b) In a pitcher or large measuring cup, dissolve the salt in the water, stirring if necessary to encourage the salt to dissolve. Pour the saltwater into the crock until the ingredients are submerged, leaving a couple of inches of room at the top for the ingredients to expand.

c) Cover with a lid or a cloth, and allow it to ferment for five to seven days, or until it has reached your desired tanginess. Remove the weights, dish out into jars or a bowl, cover, and refrigerate, where the pickles should last for six months to one year.

34.   Taco Pickles

Makes about 1 quart/liter

Ingredients:

- ½ medium cauliflower, coarsely chopped into about nickel-size pieces
- ¼ cabbage, coarsely chopped
- 1 medium carrot, coarsely chopped
- ½ jalapeño pepper, finely chopped
- ¼ red bell pepper, coarsely chopped
- ½ stalk celery, coarsely chopped
- 1 tablespoon turmeric powder
- 1 quart (or liter) filtered water
- 3 tablespoons unrefined fine sea salt or 6 tablespoons unrefined coarse sea salt

Directions:

a) In a small to medium crock, combine the cauliflower, cabbage, carrot, jalapeño, bell pepper, and celery, and toss until they are well mixed.

b) In a small bowl or pitcher, mix together the turmeric powder, water, and salt until the sea salt has dissolved. Pour the saltwater mixture over the chopped vegetables until the ingredients are submerged, leaving a couple of inches of room at the top for the ingredients to expand. Weight the vegetables with clean, food-safe weights or a jar or bowl of water to keep the vegetables submerged. Cover with a lid or a cloth, and allow it to ferment for five days.

c) Remove the weights, transfer the vegetables and some brine to jars or a bowl, cover, and refrigerate, where it should last for up to a year.

35. White Kimchi

Makes about 4 quarts

Ingredients:

- 1 large Napa cabbage (about 2½ pounds), quartered, with the stalk removed, and cut into 1-inch chunks
- 1 large carrot, julienned into 2-inch-long strips
- 1 large black Spanish radish or 3 red radishes, julienned
- 1 red bell pepper, seeded, cored, and julienned
- 3 sprigs green onion or chives, chopped into 1-inch pieces
- 2 pears (I use red pears, but you can use whatever type is available), stemmed, seeded, and quartered
- 3 garlic cloves, peeled
- ½ small onion, quartered
- 1-inch piece fresh ginger
- 3 tablespoons unrefined fine sea salt or 6 tablespoons unrefined coarse sea salt
- 6 cups filtered water

Directions:

a) In a large bowl, combine the cabbage, carrot, radish, bell pepper, and green onions.

b) Combine the pears, garlic, onion, and ginger in a food processor, and blend into a puree. Pour the pear mixture over the chopped vegetables. Add the salt, and toss all the vegetables together until they are evenly coated in the pear puree and salt.

c) Place the vegetable mixture in a large crock, and pour the water over it.

d) Place a plate that fits inside the crock to cover the vegetables and hold them submerged.

e) Place food-safe weights or a glass bowl or jar filled with water on top of the plate to keep the vegetables submerged.

f) Cover with a lid and store in a cool, undisturbed place for approximately one week or until it has reached your desired level of tanginess.

g) Transfer to jars or a bowl, cover, and refrigerate, where the kimchi should last for up to a year.

FRUIT CULTURES & VINEGARS

36. Cultured Spicy Peach Chutney

Makes approximately 2 to 3 cups

Ingredients:

- ½ small onion, chopped (about ⅓ cup chopped) and sautéed
- 2 medium peaches, pitted and coarsely chopped
- ½ teaspoon unrefined sea salt
- Pinch black pepper
- ⅛ teaspoon cloves
- ¼ teaspoon turmeric powder
- ½ teaspoon ground coriander
- ½ teaspoon cinnamon
- 1 cayenne pepper, dried and crushed
- 3 tablespoons whey, 2 probiotic capsules, or ½ teaspoon probiotic powder

Directions:

a) Combine all the ingredients in a bowl; if you're using probiotic capsules, empty the contents into the fruit mixture, and discard the empty capsule shells.

b) Toss until it is mixed well. Pour the mixture into a half-quart mason jar with a lid, cover, and leave at room temperature for approximately twelve hours.

c) Refrigerate, where it should keep for about four days.

37. Sweet Vanilla Peaches

Makes about 5 cups

Ingredients:

- 5 medium peaches, pitted and coarsely chopped (about 5 cups chopped)
- $\frac{1}{2}$ teaspoon vanilla powder
- $\frac{1}{2}$ teaspoon cardamom powder (optional)
- 1 tablespoon pure maple syrup
- 2 tablespoons whey

Directions:

a) In a large bowl, combine all the ingredients and mix well. Scoop the mixture into a 1-quart mason jar, cover, and let sit for twelve hours.

b) Refrigerate, where it should keep for four days.

38. Crabapple Vinegar

Makes about 1 quart/liter

Ingredients:

- ½ cup coconut sugar
- 1 quart (or liter) filtered water
- About 2 pounds' crabapples

Directions:

a) In a pitcher or large measuring cup, mix together the sugar and water, stirring if necessary to encourage the sugar to dissolve.

b) Place the crabapples in a thoroughly cleaned 1-quart jar with a wide mouth, leaving about 1 inch at the top of the jar. Pour the sugar-water solution over the crabapples, leaving about ¾ inch at the top of the jar. The crabapples will float to the top, and some won't be submerged, but that's okay.

c) Cover the opening with a few layers of clean cheesecloth, and attach an elastic band around the mouth of the jar or crock to hold the cheesecloth in place.

d) Every day, remove the cheesecloth and stir to cover the crabapples with the sugar-water solution, re-covering with the cheesecloth when you're done. This must be done every day to ensure that the apples don't go moldy during the fermentation process.

e) After two weeks, strain off the crabapples, reserving the liquid; you can add the crabapples to your compost. Pour the liquid into a bottle, and seal with a tight-fitting lid or cork. The vinegar keeps for approximately one year.

39. Apple Vinegar

Makes about ½ to 1 quart/liter

Ingredients:

- ½ cup coconut sugar
- 1 quart filtered water
- 4 apples, cores and skins included

Directions:

a) In a pitcher or large measuring cup, mix together the sugar and water, stirring if necessary to encourage the sugar to dissolve.

b) Chop the apples into quarters, and then chop each piece in half. Place the apple pieces, cores and skins included, in a 1- to 2-quart jar or crock, leaving about 1 to 2 inches at the top of the jar.

c) Pour the sugar-water solution over the apples, leaving about $\frac{3}{4}$ inch at the top of the jar. The apples will float to the top, and some won't be submerged, but that's okay.

d) Cover the opening with a few layers of clean cheesecloth, and attach an elastic band around the mouth of the jar or crock to hold the cheesecloth in place.

e) Every day, remove the cheesecloth, and stir to cover the apples with the sugar-water solution, re-covering with the cheesecloth when you're done. You must do every day to ensure that the apples don't go moldy during the fermentation process.

f) After two weeks, strain off the apples, reserving the liquid; you can add the apples to your compost. Pour the liquid into a bottle, and seal with a tight-fitting lid or cork. The vinegar keeps for approximately one year.

g) Push them through an electric juicer to make apple juice. If you don't have a juicer, just cut the apples into quarters and puree them in a food processor

h) hen push the apple pulp through a muslin-lined sieve or muslin bag to remove the fiber from the juice.

i) Pour the juice into clean, dark, glass jugs or bottles without putting a lid on them. Cover the tops with a few layers of cheesecloth, and hold them in place with an elastic band.

j) Store the bottles or jars in a cool, dark place for three weeks to six months.

40. Pineapple Vinegar

Makes about ½ to 1 quart/liter

Ingredients:

- ½ cup coconut sugar
- 1 quart filtered water
- 1 medium pineapple

Directions:

a) In a pitcher or large measuring cup, mix together the sugar and water, stirring if necessary to encourage the sugar to dissolve.

b) Remove the skin and core from the pineapple. Set the meat of the fruit aside for another use. Coarsely chop the skins and core. Place the pineapple scraps in a 1- to 2-quart jar or crock, leaving about 1 to 2 inches at the top of the jar.

c) Pour the sugar-water solution over the pineapple skins and core, leaving about ¾ inch at the top of the jar. The pieces will float to the top, and some won't be submerged, but that's okay.

d) Cover the opening with a few layers of clean cheesecloth, and attach an elastic band around the mouth of the jar or crock to hold the cheesecloth in place.

e) Every day, remove the cheesecloth, and stir to cover the pineapple pieces with the sugar-water solution. You must do every day to ensure that the pineapple pieces don't go moldy during the fermentation process.

f) After two weeks, strain off the pineapple pieces, reserving the liquid; you can add the pineapple to your compost. Pour the liquid into a bottle, and seal with a tight-fitting lid or cork. The vinegar keeps for approximately one year.

CULTURED BEVERAGES

41. Vegan Kefir

Makes about 1 quart/liter

Ingredients:

- 1 quart (or liter) filtered water
- ½ cup raw, unsalted cashews
- 1 teaspoon coconut sugar, pure maple syrup, or agave nectar
- 1 tablespoon kefir grains
- Mandarin sections for garnish (optional)

Directions:

a) In a blender, blend together the water, cashews, and coconut sugar (or maple syrup or agave nectar) until it is smooth and creamy.

b) Pour the cashew milk into a $1\frac{1}{2}$- to 2-quart glass jar, making sure that it is less than $2/3$ full. Add the kefir grains, stir, and place the cap on the jar.

c) Leave the jar at room temperature for twenty-four to forty-eight hours, gently agitating it periodically. The cashew milk will become somewhat bubbly, then it will begin to coagulate and separate; simply shake it to remix the kefir, or scoop out the thicker curds and use them as you would use soft cheese or sour cream.

d) Refrigerate for up to one week. When ready to serve the kefir, pour it into a glass and garnish the rim of the glass with mandarin sections, if desired.

42. Black Tea Kombucha

Makes about 3½ quarts/liters

Ingredients:

- 4 quarts (or liters) filtered water
- 1 cup unrefined sugar
- 4 black tea bags or 4 heaping teaspoons loose-leaf tea
- 1 kombucha starter culture

Directions:

a) In a large stainless-steel pot, bring the water to a boil, add the sugar, and stir until the sugar is fully dissolved.

b) Add the black tea bags or loose tea, and boil for an additional 10 minutes to kill off any unwanted microbes that may be present on the tea bags.

c) Turn off the heat, and allow the tea to steep for 15 minutes; remove the tea bags.

d) Allow the tea to cool to room temperature or slightly lukewarm temperature; it should be no warmer than about 70°F or 21°C to ensure that the kombucha culture is not damaged.

e) Pour the steeped tea into a large ceramic crock or wide-mouthed glass water jug, such as those used to make iced tea.

f) Add to the tea the kombucha starter culture along with any tea it came with.

g) Cover the top of the crock or jug with a piece of clean linen or cotton (avoid using cheesecloth, as it is too porous), and attach an elastic band around the rim to hold the cloth in place; alternatively, you can use tape around the edge to hold the cloth in place and ensure that the cloth doesn't fall into the crock or jug.

h) Place the crock or jug someplace quiet with air ventilation, in a warm but not sunlit area, where it will not be disturbed.

i) The ideal fermentation temperature range is 73 to 82°F, or 23 to 28°C. Once you've located a spot for it, do not move the crock or jug while the kombucha is fermenting, as it may interfere with the culturing process.

j) Wait about five to six days to harvest your kombucha. First, check the taste: If it is sweeter than you'd like, allow it to ferment another day or two. If it has a vinegary taste, you may need to bottle future batches after fermenting a shorter period of time; it is still fine to drink, but you may need to dilute it with water when you drink it to avoid irritating your throat or stomach.

k) Pour all but approximately 2 cups of your fermented kombucha into a glass jar, a container with a lid, or multiple single-serving resealable glass jars (old-fashioned soda pop bottles with the flip-top lid work well), cover, and store it in the refrigerator.

43. African Red Tea Kombucha

Makes about 3½ quarts/liters

Ingredients:

- 4 quarts filtered water
- 1 cup coconut sugar
- 4 teaspoons rooibos loose-leaf tea or 4 rooibos tea bags
- 1 kombucha starter culture

Directions:

a) In a large stainless-steel pot, bring the water to a boil, add the sugar, and stir until the sugar is fully dissolved.

b) Add the rooibos tea bags or loose tea, and boil for an additional 10 minutes to kill off any unwanted microbes that may be present on the tea bags. Turn off the heat, and allow the tea to steep for 15 minutes; remove the tea bags.

c) Let the tea cool to room temperature or slightly lukewarm temperature; it should be no warmer than about 70°F or 21°C to ensure that the kombucha culture is not damaged.

d) Pour the steeped tea into a large ceramic crock or wide-mouthed glass water jug, through a fine-mesh sieve in order to remove any loose-leaf tea (if using).

e) Add to the tea the kombucha starter culture along with any tea it came with. Cover the top of the crock or jug with a piece of clean linen or cotton (avoid using cheesecloth, as it is too porous), and attach an elastic band around the rim to hold the cloth in place; alternatively, you can use tape around the edge to hold the cloth in place and ensure that the cloth doesn't fall into the crock or jug.

f) Place the crock or jug someplace quiet with air ventilation, in a warm but not sunlit area, where it will not be disturbed. The ideal fermentation temperature range is 73 to 82°F, or 23 to 28°C. Once you've located a spot for it, do not move the crock or jug while the kombucha is fermenting, as it may interfere with the culturing process.

g) Wait about five to six days to harvest your kombucha. First, check the taste: If it is sweeter than you'd like, allow it to ferment another day or two. If it has a vinegary taste, you may need to bottle future batches after a shorter period of time; it is still fine to drink, but you may need to dilute it with water when you drink it to avoid irritating your throat or stomach.

h) Pour all but approximately 2 cups of your fermented kombucha into a glass jar or container with a lid, or multiple single-serving resealable glass jars (old-fashioned soda pop bottles with the flip-top lid work well), cover, and store it in the refrigerator.

i) To increase its fizziness, add a pinch of sugar, and wait another a day or two to drink it. If you keep it longer than a week, you may need to loosen the lid in the fridge to allow gases to escape and prevent the glass from breaking due to excess pressure that may occur over longer periods of time.

44. Cultured Bloody Mary

Makes about 2 cups

Ingredients:

- 4 medium tomatoes
- Juice from ½ lime
- ⅓ cup brine from kimchi, sauerkraut, or pickles
- Dash unrefined sea salt
- Dash pepper
- 1 stalk celery (optional, for garnish)

Directions:

a) In a blender, combine all the ingredients except the celery, and blend until it is smooth.

b) Pour the mixture into a covered glass dish, and allow it to ferment for two to twelve hours, depending on your preference; longer fermentation times result in a tangier drink.

c) Garnish with celery if desired, and serve immediately.

d) Store any leftovers in a jar in the fridge for up to three days.

FERMENTED DESSERTS

45.   Tzatziki

Makes about 1½ to 2 cups

Ingredients:

- 1 cup raw, unsalted cashews
- ½ cup filtered water
- 1 probiotic capsule or ¼ teaspoon probiotic powder
- Juice from 1 lemon
- 1 garlic clove, minced
- 2 tablespoons minced onion
- 1 teaspoon unrefined sea salt
- One 3-inch piece of a medium cucumber

Directions:

a) In a small to medium glass bowl, combine the cashews and water. Empty the contents of the probiotic capsule (discarding the empty capsule shell) or probiotic powder into the cashew mixture, and stir to combine. Cover and set aside for twenty-four hours.

b) In a blender, combine the cashew mixture with the lemon juice, garlic, onion, and salt, and blend until smooth and creamy; return the mixture to the bowl. Grate the cucumber, add it to the cashew mixture, and stir until combined. Store, covered, in the refrigerator for up to three days.

c) When ready to serve, garnish with cucumber slices and/or slivers, if desired.

46. Creamy French Onion Dip

Makes about 2½ cups

Ingredients:

- 2 cups raw, unsalted cashews
- 1½ cups filtered water
- 2 probiotic capsules or ½ teaspoon probiotic powder
- Juice from ½ lemon
- 2 tablespoons minced green onion
- 2 tablespoons minced fresh parsley
- About 1 teaspoon unrefined sea salt, or to taste
- Chives or spring onions for garnish (optional)

Directions:

a) In a small to medium glass bowl, combine the cashews and water.

b) Empty the contents of the probiotic capsules (discarding the empty capsule shells) or probiotic powder into the cashews, and stir to mix.

c) Cover and allow the mixture to culture for twenty-four to forty-eight hours.

d) When ready to serve, garnish with chives or spring onions, if desired.

47. Green Salad with Peaches & Chèvre

Serves 2 to 4

Ingredients:

Salad

- 1 small package mixed greens
- 2 to 3 fresh peaches, pitted and halved
- 1 tablespoon extra-virgin olive oil
- 1-inch round Chèvre

Dressing

- ¾ cup extra-virgin olive oil
- ⅓ cup apple cider vinegar
- ½ teaspoon unrefined sea salt
- ½ teaspoon dried basil
- ½ teaspoon dried thyme
- 1 teaspoon pure maple syrup or agave nectar

Directions:

Preheat your barbecue to 300 to 350°F, or heat a cast-iron grill pan on your stovetop over low to medium heat.

Wash and dry the mesclun greens, and place in a large bowl; set aside.

Brush the peach halves with olive oil, and place flat side down on the barbecue or grill pan. Grill for about 3 minutes, or until peaches are soft but not mushy. Remove the peaches from the grill, turn off the heat, and set aside.

Cut the Chèvre into discs, and set aside.

In a blender, combine all dressing ingredients, and blend until smooth. Pour your desired amount of dressing over the mixed greens, and toss the salad until it is well coated. Store any leftover dressing in a covered jar for up to one week.

Top the salad with the Chèvre discs and grilled peach halves, and serve in large bowls or on plates.

48. Coconut Cream Cheese

Ingredients:

- One 13.5-ounce can coconut milk
- 1 probiotic capsule or ¼ teaspoon probiotic powder
- 1 to 2 teaspoons pure maple syrup
- 1 teaspoon vanilla powder or pure vanilla extract
- 1 teaspoon lemon zest (optional)

Directions:

a) Open the can of coconut milk. If the coconut cream and water have already separated, scoop off the thick cream into a small bowl.

b) If it has not separated, in a small bowl simply mix both the coconut cream and coconut water together until smooth.

c) Add the contents of the probiotic capsule (discarding the empty capsule shell) or probiotic powder, and mix together.

d) Cover with a lid or cloth, and allow it to sit undisturbed for eight to ten hours in a warm setting (approximately 110 to 115°F or 43 to 46°C, but don't worry if it's not quite within that range).

e) After it has cultured, refrigerate for at least one to two hours. If the coconut cream and water have separated, scoop off the thickened coconut cream for use.

f) Add the maple syrup, vanilla powder or extract, and lemon zest if desired. Stir together until smooth. Use immediately as an icing for cakes, cupcakes, or other baked goods.

g) Lasts about one week, covered, in the fridge.

49. Pear Crêpes with Macadamia Cheese

Makes 8 large crêpes

Ingredients:

Crêpes

- 2 tablespoons olive oil, plus more for oiling frying pan
- 1½ cups all-purpose gluten-free flour (I use Bob's Red Mill xanthan-free flour)
- 1½ cups almond milk
- 2 tablespoons finely ground flaxseed whisked into 6 tablespoons water
- 1 teaspoon baking soda
- Pinch unrefined sea salt
- Cardamom Pear Topping
- 4 medium pears, cored and sliced
- Pinch ground cardamom
- ½ cup filtered water, divided
- 2 tablespoons organic cane sugar
- 1 tablespoon tapioca flour

Cream Cheese Topping

- Macadamia Cream Cheese

Directions:

a) For the crêpe batter, in a large bowl combine the 2 tablespoons oil, flour, almond milk, flaxseed-water mixture, baking soda, and salt; whisk together.

b) In a large frying pan over medium heat, add enough oil to grease the entire bottom of the pan, and pour enough crêpe batter to thinly coat the pan. Cook for approximately 1 minute or until the bubbles disappear, and flip. Repeat with the remaining batter until the batter is all used up.

c) For the topping, in a medium frying pan over low to medium heat, add the pears, cardamom, and $\frac{1}{4}$ cup of the water. Cook for approximately 5 minutes or until the pears are slightly softened. In a small glass bowl, combine the remaining $\frac{1}{4}$ cup of water, sugar, and tapioca until they are well mixed.

d) Add the sugar-tapioca mixture to the pears, stirring constantly. Allow to cook for another minute or until the sauce has thickened.

e) Top each crêpe with $\frac{1}{8}$ of the pear mixture and $\frac{1}{8}$ of the macadamia cream cheese. Serve immediately.

50. Gingerbread Cookie Ice Cream Sandwiches

Makes about 24 cookies or 12 ice cream sandwiches

Ingredients:

- ½ cup coconut oil
- ½ cup coconut sugar
- ¼ cup molasses
- 1 tablespoon finely ground flaxseed whisked into 3 tablespoons water
- 1 cup brown rice flour
- 1 cup millet flour
- 1½ teaspoons baking soda
- 2 teaspoons ground ginger
- 1 teaspoon ground cinnamon
- ¼ teaspoon ground nutmeg
- Cultured Vanilla Ice Cream

Directions:

a) Preheat your oven to 350°F.

b) In a mixer, combine the oil and sugar, and begin mixing. While they're still blending, add the molasses, flaxseed-water mixture, brown rice flour, millet flour, baking soda, ginger, cinnamon, and nutmeg, and continue to mix until the mixture forms a soft, pliable dough.

c) Form the dough into balls approximately $1\frac{1}{2}$ inches in diameter, or the size of a walnut. Press them firmly with the palm of your hand onto a parchment-lined baking sheet to form 2-inch disks, leaving space between the cookies for them to spread. Bake for 8 minutes or until they are firm but not hard. Let cool on wire racks.

d) Once the gingerbread cookies have cooled, spoon the cultured vanilla ice cream onto one of the cookies, and press another cookie onto it to form a sandwich. Repeat for the remaining cookies. Freeze or serve immediately. If freezing, allow the ice cream sandwiches to sit at room temperature for about 10 minutes before serving.

51. Cultured Vanilla Ice Cream

Ingredients:

- 1 cup raw, unsalted cashews
- 2 cups almond milk
- 1 probiotic capsule or $\frac{1}{4}$ teaspoon probiotic powder
- 5 large fresh Medjool dates, pitted
- 1 teaspoon vanilla powder

Directions:

a) In a small bowl, combine the cashews and 1 cup of milk; add the contents of the probiotic capsule (discarding the empty capsule shell) or probiotic powder, and mix well.

b) Cover and let sit for eight to twelve hours, depending on your taste preference; longer fermentation times create a tangier flavor.

c) In a blender, combine the cashew mixture, dates, and vanilla powder, and blend until smooth. Pour into an ice cream machine, and follow the manufacturer's directions to process into ice cream (usually 20 to 25 minutes).

52. Pumpkin Pie Ice Cream

Makes about 1 quart/liter

Ingredients:

- ½ cup raw, unsalted cashews
- ¼ cup filtered water
- 2 probiotic capsules, or ½ teaspoon probiotic powder
- 2 cups almond milk
- 2 cups cooked squash
- 7 fresh Medjool dates, pitted
- 1½ teaspoons ground cinnamon
- ½ teaspoon ground ginger
- ½ teaspoon ground cloves
- ⅛ teaspoon nutmeg

Directions:

a) In a small bowl, mix the cashews and water; add the contents of the probiotic capsule (discarding the empty capsule shell) or probiotic powder, and mix well. Cover and let sit for twelve hours.

b) In a blender, combine the cashew mixture with the milk, squash, dates, cinnamon, ginger. cloves, and nutmeg, and blend until the mixture is smooth. Pour it into an ice cream maker, and follow the manufacturer's instructions. Serve immediately.

53. Black Cherry Ice Cream

Makes about 1 quart/liter

Ingredients:

- 1 cup raw, unsalted cashews
- 1 cup filtered water
- 1 probiotic capsule or ¼ teaspoon probiotic powder
- 2 cups fresh black cherries, pitted and stems removed (if using frozen cherries, allow to thaw before using), plus a few more for garnish (optional)
- 1¼ cup almond milk
- 4 fresh medjool dates, pitted

Directions:

a) In a medium bowl, soak cashews in the water for eight hours or overnight.

b) Pour the cashews and water into a blender, and blend until the mixture is smooth and creamy. Pour it into a small glass dish with a lid. Empty the probiotic capsule (discarding the empty capsule shell) or probiotic powder into the cashew mixture, and stir together. Cover it with a lid or clean cloth, and allow it to ferment for eight to twelve hours.

c) In a blender or food processor, combine the cashew mixture with the cherries, milk, and dates, and blend until smooth. Pour the mixture into an ice cream maker, and follow the manufacturer's directions to process into ice cream. Garnish with additional cherries if desired, and serve immediately.

54.   Orange Creamsicle Cheesecake

Makes one 12-inch cheesecake

Ingredients:

Crust

- 1 cup raw, unsalted almonds
- 3 fresh Medjool dates, pitted
- 1 tablespoon coconut oil
- Pinch unrefined sea salt

Filling

- 2 cups raw, unsalted cashews
- 1 cup filtered water
- 1 probiotic capsule or $\frac{1}{4}$ teaspoon probiotic powder
- 3 cups orange juice
- 2 tablespoons pure maple syrup
- 1 teaspoon vanilla powder
- 1 cup coconut oil
- $\frac{1}{4}$ cup plus 1 tablespoon lecithin (5 tablespoons)
- Thin slices of orange, with peel, for garnish (optional)

Directions:

a) For the crust, in a food processor, combine all crust ingredients, and blend until finely chopped. Transfer to a 12-inch springform pan, and press over the bottom surface of the pan until it is firm.

b) For the filling, in a medium bowl, combine the cashews, water, and the contents of the probiotic capsule (discarding the empty capsule shell) or probiotic powder; stir until combined. Cover with a lid or clean cloth, and let sit for twelve to twenty-four hours to culture.

c) In a blender, combine the cashew mixture with the orange juice, maple syrup, vanilla powder, oil, and lecithin, and blend until smooth.

d) Pour the mixture over the crust. Refrigerate for four to six hours, or until set. Garnish with orange slices if desired, and serve. The cheesecake lasts approximately four days in the refrigerator in a covered container.

55. Pomegranate Cheesecake

Makes one 12-inch cheesecake

Ingredients:

Crust

- 1 cup raw, unsalted hazelnuts
- 4 fresh Medjool dates, pitted
- 1 tablespoon coconut oil
- Pinch unrefined sea salt

Filling

- 2 cups raw, unsalted cashews
- 1 cup filtered water
- 1 probiotic capsule or ¼ teaspoon probiotic powder
- 3 cups pomegranate juice
- 2 tablespoons pure maple syrup or agave nectar
- 1 teaspoon vanilla powder
- 1 cup coconut oil
- ¼ cup plus 2 tablespoons lecithin (6 tablespoons)

- Fresh pomegranate arils (seeds) to garnish (optional)

Directions:

a) For the crust, in a food processor, combine all crust ingredients, and blend until finely chopped. Transfer to a 12-inch springform pan, and press over the bottom surface of the pan until it is firm.

b) For the filling, in a medium bowl, combine the cashews, water, and the contents of the probiotic capsule (discarding the empty capsule shell) or probiotic powder. Stir the mixture until it is combined. Cover with a lid or clean cloth, and let sit for twelve to twenty-four hours to culture.

c) In a blender, combine the cashew mixture with the pomegranate juice, maple syrup or agave nectar, vanilla powder, oil, and lecithin, and blend until smooth.

d) Pour the mixture over the crust. Refrigerate for four to six hours, or until set. Top with fresh pomegranate arils if desired. Serve.

e) The cheesecake lasts approximately four days in the refrigerator in a covered container.

56. Blackberry Cheesecake

Makes one 12-inch cheesecake

Ingredients:

Crust

- 1 cup raw, unsalted almonds
- 3 fresh Medjool dates, pitted
- 1 tablespoon coconut oil
- Pinch unrefined sea salt

Filling

- 2 cups raw, unsalted cashews
- 1 cup filtered water
- 1 probiotic capsule or $\frac{1}{4}$ teaspoon probiotic powder
- $\frac{1}{4}$ cup plus 1 tablespoon pure maple syrup (5 tablespoons)
- 1 teaspoon vanilla powder
- $\frac{1}{2}$ cup coconut oil
- $\frac{1}{2}$ cup lecithin
- 2 cups almond milk

Directions:

a) 2½ cups fresh blackberries (if using frozen, allow them to thaw before making the cheesecake), plus more for garnish.

b) For the crust, in a food processor, combine all crust ingredients, and blend until finely chopped. Transfer to a 12-inch springform pan, and press over the bottom surface of the pan until it is firm.

c) For the filling, in a medium bowl, combine the cashews, water, and the contents of the probiotic capsule (discarding the empty capsule shell) or probiotic powder; stir the mixture until it is combined. Cover with a lid or clean cloth, and let sit for twenty-four to forty-eight hours to culture.

d) In a blender, combine the cashew mixture with the maple syrup, vanilla powder, oil, lecithin, and milk, and blend until smooth. Add the blackberries, and blend until smooth.

e) Pour the mixture over the crust. Refrigerate for four to six hours, or until set. Garnish with additional blackberries, if desired, and serve. The cheesecake lasts approximately four days in the refrigerator in a covered container.

FERMENTED VEGGIES

57.   Dill pickles

Ingredients:

- 4 lbs. of 4-inch pickling cucumber
- 2 Tablespoons dill seed or 4 to 5 heads fresh or dry dill wee
- 1/2 cup salt
- 1/4 cup vinegar (5%
- 8 cups water and one or more of the following ingredients:
- 2 cloves garlic (optional)
- 2 dried red peppers (optional)
- 2 teaspoons whole mixed pickling spices

Directions:

a) Wash cucumbers. Cut 1/16-inch slice of blossom end and discard. Leave 1/4-inch of stem attached. Place half of dill and spices on bottom of a clean, suitable container.

b) Add cucumbers, remaining dill, and spices. Dissolve salt in vinegar and water and pour over cucumbers.

c) Add suitable cover and weight. Store where temperature is between 70° and 75°F for about 3 to 4 weeks while fermenting. Temperatures of 55° to 65°F are acceptable, but the fermentation will take 5 to 6 weeks.

d) Avoid temperatures above 80°F, or pickles will become too soft during fermentation. Fermenting pickles cure slowly. Check the container several times a week and promptly remove surface scum or mold. Caution: If the pickles become soft, slimy, or develop a disagreeable odor, discard them.

e) Fully fermented pickles may be stored in the original container for about 4 to 6 months, provided they are refrigerated and surface scum and molds are removed regularly. Canning fully fermented pickles is a better way to store them. To can them, pour the brine into a pan, heat slowly to a boil, and simmer 5 minutes. Filter brine through paper coffee filters to reduce cloudiness, if desired.

f) Fill hot jar with pickles and hot brine, leaving 1/2-inch headspace.

g) Remove air bubbles and adjust headspace if needed. Wipe rims of jars with a dampened clean paper towel.

58.   Sauerkraut

Ingredients:

- 25 lbs. cabbage
- 3/4 cup canning or pickling salt

Yield: About 9 quarts

Directions:

a) Work with about 5 pounds of cabbage at a time. Discard outer leaves. Rinse heads under cold running water and drain. Cut heads in quarters and remove cores. Shred or slice to a thickness of a quarter.

b) Put cabbage in a suitable fermentation container and add 3 tablespoons of salt. Mix thoroughly, using clean hands. Pack firmly until salt draws juices from cabbage.

c) Repeat shredding, salting, and packing until all cabbage is in the container. Be sure it is deep enough so that its rim is at least 4 or 5 inches above the cabbage. If juice does not cover cabbage, add boiled and cooled brine (1-1/2 tablespoons of salt per quart of water).

d) Add plate and weights; cover container with a clean bath towel.

e) If you weigh the cabbage down with a brine-filled bag, do not disturb the crock until normal fermentation is completed (when bubbling ceases). If you use jars as weight, you will have to check the kraut two to three times each week and remove scum if it forms. Fully fermented kraut may be kept tightly covered in the refrigerator for several months.

f) Remove air bubbles and adjust headspace if needed. Wipe rims of jars with a dampened clean paper towel.

59. Bread-and-butter pickles

Ingredients:

- 6 lbs. of 4- to 5-inch pickling cucumbers
- 8 cups thinly sliced onions
- 1/2 cup canning or pickling salt
- 4 cups vinegar (5%)
- 4-1/2 cups sugar
- 2 Tablespoons mustard seed
- 1-1/2 Tablespoons celery seed
- 1 Tablespoon ground turmeric
- 1 cup pickling lime

Yield: About 8 pints

Directions:

a) Wash cucumbers. Cut 1/16-inch of blossom end and discard. Cut into 3/16-inch slices. Combine cucumbers and onions in a large bowl. Add salt. Cover with 2 inches crushed or cubed ice. Refrigerate 3 to 4 hours, adding more ice as needed.

b) Combine remaining ingredients in a large pot. Boil 10 minutes. Drain and add cucumbers and onions and slowly reheat to boiling. Fill hot pint jars with slices and cooking syrup, leaving 1/2-inch headspace.

c) Remove air bubbles and adjust headspace if needed. Wipe rims of jars with a dampened clean paper towel.

60. Dill pickles

Ingredients:

- 8 lbs. of 3- to 5-inch pickling cucumbers
- 2 gallons water
- 1-1/4 cups canning or pickling salt
- 1-1/2 quarts vinegar (5%)
- 1/4 cup sugar
- 2 quarts water
- 2 Tablespoons whole mixed pickling spice
- about 3 Tablespoons whole mustard seed
- about 14 heads of fresh dill

Yield: About 7 to 9 pints

Directions:

a) Wash cucumbers. Cut 1/16-inch slice of blossom end and discard, but leave 1/4-inch of stem attached. Dissolve 3/4 cup salt in 2 gallons water. Pour over cucumbers and let stand 12 hours. Drain.

b) Combine vinegar, 1/2 cup salt, sugar, and 2 quarts water. Add mixed pickling spices tied in a clean white cloth. Heat to boiling. Fill hot jars with cucumbers.

c) Add 1 teaspoon mustard seed and 1-1/2 heads fresh dill per pint. Cover with boiling pickling solution, leaving 1/2-inch head-space. Remove air bubbles and adjust headspace if needed. Wipe rims of jars with a dampened clean paper towel.

61. Sweet gherkin pickles

Ingredients:

- 7 lbs. cucumbers (1-1/2 inch or less)
- 1/2 cup canning or pickling salt
- 8 cups sugar
- 6 cups vinegar (5%)
- 3/4 teaspoons turmeric
- 2 teaspoons celery seeds
- 2 teaspoons whole mixed pickling spice
- 2 cinnamon sticks
- 1/2 teaspoons fennel (optional)
- 2 teaspoons vanilla (optional)

Yield: About 6 to 7 pints

Directions:

a) Wash cucumbers. Cut 1/16-inch slice of blossom end and discard, but leave 1/4-inch of stem attached.

b) Place cucumbers in large container and cover with boiling water. Six to 8 hours later, and again on the second day, drain and cover with 6 quarts of fresh boiling water containing 1/4-cup salt. On the third day, drain and prick cucumbers with a table fork.

c) Combine and bring to a boil 3 cups vinegar, 3 cups sugar, turmeric, and spices. Pour over cucumbers. Six to 8 hours later, drain and save the pickling syrup. Add another 2 cups each of sugar and vinegar and reheat to boil. Pour over pickles.

d) On the fourth day, drain and save syrup. Add another 2 cups sugar and 1 cup vinegar. Heat to boiling and pour over pickles. Drain and save pickling syrup 6 to 8 hours later. Add 1 cup sugar and 2 teaspoons vanilla and heat to boiling.

e) Fill hot sterile pint jars with pickles and cover with hot syrup, leaving 1/2-inch headspace.

f) Remove air bubbles and adjust headspace if needed. Wipe rims of jars with a dampened clean paper towel.

62. 14-Day sweet pickles

Ingredients:

- 4 lbs. of 2- to 5-inch pickling cucumbers
- 3/4 cup canning or pickling salt
- 2 teaspoons celery seed
- 2 Tablespoons mixed pickling spices
- 5-1/2 cups sugar
- 4 cups vinegar (5%)

Yield: About 5 to 9 pints

Directions:

a) Wash cucumbers. Cut 1/16-inch slice of blossom end and discard, but leave 1/4-inch of stem attached. Place whole cucumbers in suitable 1-gallon container.

b) Add 1/4 cup canning or pickling salt to 2 quarts water and bring to a boil. Pour over cucumbers. Add suitable cover and weight.

c) Place clean towel over container and keep the temperature at about 70°F. On the third and fifth days, drain salt water and discard. Rinse cucumbers and return cucumbers to container. Add 1/4 cup salt to 2 quarts fresh water and boil. Pour over cucumbers.

d) Replace cover and weight, and re-cover with clean towel. On the seventh day, drain salt water and discard. Rinse cucumbers, cover, and weight.

63. Quick sweet pickles

Ingredients:

- 8 lbs. of 3- to 4-inch pickling cucumbers
- 1/3 cup canning or pickling salt
- 4-1/2 cups sugar
- 3-1/2 cups vinegar (5%)
- 2 teaspoons celery seed
- 1 Tablespoon whole allspice
- 2 Tablespoons mustard seed
- 1 cup pickling lime (optional)

Yield: About 7 to 9 pints

Directions:

a) Wash cucumbers. Cut 1/16-inch of blossom end and discard, but leave 1/4 inch of stem attached. Slice or cut in strips, if desired. Place in bowl and sprinkle with 1/3 cup salt. Cover with 2 inches of crushed or cubed ice.

b) Refrigerate 3 to 4 hours. Add more ice as needed. Drain well.

c) Combine sugar, vinegar, celery seed, allspice, and mustard seed in 6-quart kettle. Heat to boiling.

d) Hot pack—Add cucumbers and heat slowly until vinegar solution returns to boil. Stir occasionally to make sure mixture heats evenly. Fill sterile jars, leaving 1/2-inch headspace.

e) Raw pack—Fill hot jars, leaving 1/2-inch headspace. Add hot pickling syrup, leaving 1/2-inch headspace.

f) Remove air bubbles and adjust headspace if needed. Wipe rims of jars with a dampened clean paper towel.

64. Pickled asparagus

Ingredients:

- 10 lbs. asparagus
- 6 large garlic cloves
- 4-1/2 cups water
- 4-1/2 cups white distilled vinegar (5%)
- 6 small hot peppers (optional)
- 1/2 cup canning salt
- 3 teaspoons dill seed

Yield: 6 wide-mouth pint jars

Directions:

a) Wash asparagus well, but gently, under running water. Cut stems from the bottom to leave spears with tips that it into the canning jar, leaving a little more than 1/2-inch headspace. Peel and wash garlic cloves.

b) Place a garlic clove at the bottom of each jar, and tightly pack asparagus into hot jars with the blunt ends down. In an 8-quart saucepot, combine water, vinegar, hot peppers (optional), salt and dill seed.

c) Bring to a boil. Place one hot pepper (if used) in each jar over asparagus spears. Pour boiling hot pickling brine over spears, leaving 1/2-inch headspace.

d) Remove air bubbles and adjust headspace if needed. Wipe rims of jars with a dampened clean paper towel.

65. Pickled dilled beans

Ingredients:

- 4 lbs. fresh tender green or yellow beans
- 8 to 16 heads fresh dill
- 8 cloves garlic (optional)
- 1/2 cup canning or pickling salt
- 4 cups white vinegar (5%)
- 4 cups water
- 1 teaspoon hot red pepper flakes

Yield: About 8 pints

Directions:

a) Wash and trim ends from beans and cut to 4-inch lengths. In each hot sterile pint jar, place 1 to 2 dill heads and, if desired, 1 clove of garlic. Place whole beans upright in jars, leaving 1/2-inch headspace.

b) Trim beans to ensure proper it, if necessary. Combine salt, vinegar, water, and pepper flakes (if desired). Bring to a boil. Add hot solution to beans, leaving 1/2-inch headspace.

c) Remove air bubbles and adjust headspace if needed. Wipe rims of jars with a dampened clean paper towel.

66. Pickled three-bean salad

Ingredients:

- 1-1/2 cups blanched green/yellow beans
- 1-1/2 cups canned, drained, red kidney beans
- 1 cup canned, drained garbanzo beans
- 1/2 cup peeled and thinly sliced onion
- 1/2 cup trimmed and thinly sliced celery
- 1/2 cup sliced green peppers
- 1/2 cup white vinegar (5%)
- 1/4 cup bottled lemon juice
- 3/4 cup sugar
- 1/4 cup oil
- 1/2 teaspoons canning or pickling salt
- 1-1/4 cups water

Yield: About 5 to 6 half-pints

Directions:

a) Wash and snap of ends of fresh beans. Cut or snap into 1- to 2-inch pieces.

b) Blanch 3 minutes and cool immediately. Rinse kidney beans with tap water and drain again. Prepare and measure all other vegetables.

c) Combine vinegar, lemon juice, sugar, and water and bring to a boil. Remove from heat.

d) Add oil and salt and mix well. Add beans, onions, celery, and green pepper to solution and bring to a simmer.

e) Marinate 12 to 14 hours in refrigerator, then heat entire mixture to a boil. Fill hot jars with solids. Add hot liquid, leaving 1/2-inch headspace.

f) Remove air bubbles and adjust headspace if needed. Wipe rims of jars with a dampened clean paper towel.

67. Pickled beets

Ingredients:

- 7 lbs. of 2- to 2-1/2-inch diameter beets
- 4 cups vinegar (5%)
- 1-1/2 teaspoons canning or pickling salt
- 2 cups sugar
- 2 cups water
- 2 cinnamon sticks
- 12 whole cloves
- 4 to 6 onions (2- to 2-1/2-inch diameter),

Yield: About 8 pints

Directions:

a) Trim of beet tops, leaving 1 inch of stem and roots to prevent bleeding of color.

b) Wash thoroughly. Sort for size. Cover similar sizes together with boiling water and cook until tender (about 25 to 30 minutes). Caution: Drain and discard liquid. Cool beets. Trim of roots and stems and slip of skins. Slice into 1/4-inch slices. Peel and thinly slice onions.

c) Combine vinegar, salt, sugar, and fresh water. Put spices in cheesecloth bag and add to vinegar mixture. Bring to a boil. Add beets and onions. Simmer 5 minutes. Remove spice bag.

d) Fill hot jars with beets and onions, leaving 1/2-inch headspace. Add hot vinegar solution, allowing 1/2-inch headspace.

e) Remove air bubbles and adjust headspace if needed. Wipe rims of jars with a dampened clean paper towel.

68. Pickled carrots

Ingredients:

- 2-3/4 lbs. peeled carrots
- 5-1/2 cups white vinegar (5%)
- 1 cup water
- 2 cups sugar
- 2 teaspoons canning salt
- 8 teaspoons mustard seed
- 4 teaspoons celery seed

Yield: About 4 pints

Directions:

a) Wash and peel carrots. Cut into rounds that are approximately 1/2-inch thick.

b) Combine vinegar, water, sugar and canning salt in an 8-quart Dutch oven or stockpot. Bring to a boil and boil 3 minutes. Add carrots and bring back to a boil. Then reduce heat to a simmer and heat until half-cooked (about 10 minutes).

c) Meanwhile, place 2 teaspoons mustard seed and 1 tea-spoon celery seed into each empty hot pint jar. Fill jars with hot carrots, leaving 1-inch headspace. Fill with hot pickling liquid, leaving 1/2-inch headspace.

d) Remove air bubbles and adjust headspace if needed. Wipe rims of jars with a dampened clean paper towel.

69. Pickled cauliflower/Brussels

Ingredients:

- 12 cups of 1- to 2-inch cauliflower flowerets or small Brussels sprouts
- 4 cups white vinegar (5%)
- 2 cups sugar
- 2 cups thinly sliced onions
- 1 cup diced sweet red peppers
- 2 Tablespoons mustard seed
- 1 Tablespoon celery seed
- 1 teaspoon turmeric
- 1 teaspoon hot red pepper lakes

Yield: About 9 half-pints

Directions:

a) Wash cauliflower flowerets or Brussels sprouts and boil in salt water (4 teaspoons canning salt per gallon of water) for 3 minutes for cauliflower and 4 minutes for Brussels sprouts. Drain and cool.

b) Combine vinegar, sugar, onion, diced red pepper, and spices in large saucepan. Bring to a boil and simmer 5 minutes.

c) Distribute onion and diced pepper among jars. Fill hot jars with pieces and pickling solution, leaving 1/2-inch head-space.

d) Remove air bubbles and adjust headspace if needed. Wipe rims of jars with a dampened clean paper towel.

70. Chayote and jicama slaw

Ingredients:

- 4 cups julienned jicama
- 4 cups julienned chayote
- 2 cups chopped red bell pepper
- 2 chopped hot peppers
- 2-1/2 cups water
- 2-1/2 cups cider vinegar (5%)
- 1/2 cup white sugar
- 3-1/2 teaspoons canning salt
- 1 teaspoon celery seed (optional)

Yield: About 6 half-pints

Directions:

a) Caution: Wear plastic or rubber gloves and do not touch your face while handling or cutting hot peppers. If you do not wear gloves, wash hands thoroughly with soap and water before touching your face or eyes.

b) Wash, peel and thinly julienne jicama and chayote, discarding the seed of the chayote. In an 8-quart Dutch oven or stockpot, combine all ingredients except chayote. Bring to a boil and boil for 5 minutes.

c) Reduce heat to simmering and add chayote. Bring back to a boil and then turn heat of. Fill hot solids into hot half-pint jars, leaving 1/2-inch headspace.

d) Cover with boiling cooking liquid, leaving 1/2-inch headspace.

e) Remove air bubbles and adjust headspace if needed. Wipe rims of jars with a dampened clean paper towel.

71. Bread-and-butter pickled jicama

Ingredients:

- 14 cups cubed jicama
- 3 cups thinly sliced onion
- 1 cup chopped red bell pepper
- 4 cups white vinegar (5%)
- 4-1/2 cups sugar
- 2 Tablespoons mustard seed
- 1 Tablespoon celery seed
- 1 teaspoon ground turmeric

Yield: About 6 pints

Directions:

a) Combine vinegar, sugar and spices in a 12-quart Dutch oven or large saucepot. Stir and bring to a boil. Stir in prepared jicama, onion slices, and red bell pepper. Return to a boil, reduce heat and simmer 5 minutes. Stir occasionally.

b) Fill hot solids into hot pint jars, leaving 1/2-inch headspace. Cover with boiling cooking liquid, leaving 1/2-inch headspace.

c) Remove air bubbles and adjust headspace if needed. Wipe rims of jars with a dampened clean paper towel.

72.   Marinated whole mushrooms

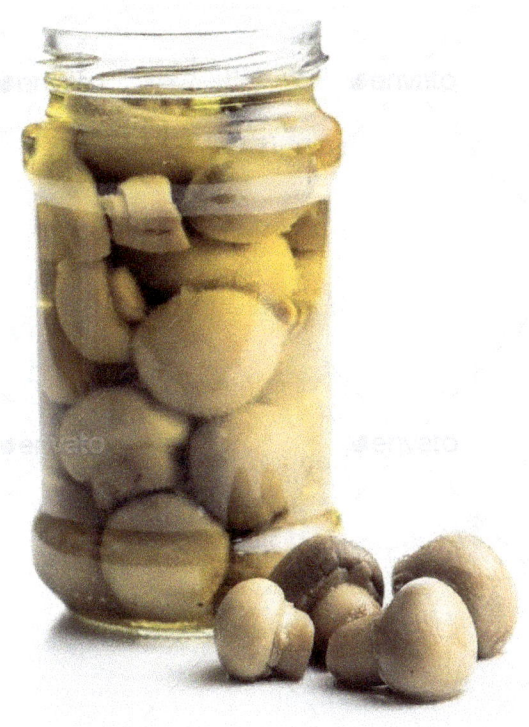

Ingredients:

- 7 lbs. small whole mushrooms
- 1/2 cup bottled lemon juice
- 2 cups olive or salad oil
- 2-1/2 cups white vinegar (5%)
- 1 Tablespoon oregano leaves
- 1 Tablespoon dried basil leaves
- 1 Tablespoon canning or pickling salt
- 1/2 cup chopped onions
- 1/4 cup diced pimiento
- 2 cloves garlic, cut in quarters
- 25 black peppercorns

Yield: About 9 half-pints

Directions:

a) Select very fresh unopened mushrooms with caps less than 1-1/4 inch in diameter. Wash. Cut stems, leaving 1/4 inch attached to cap. Add lemon juice and water to cover. Bring to boil. Simmer 5 minutes. Drain mushrooms.

b) Mix olive oil, vinegar, oregano, basil, and salt in a saucepan. Stir in onions and pimiento and heat to boiling.

c) Place 1/4 garlic clove and 2-3 peppercorns in a half-pint jar. Fill hot jars with mushrooms and hot, well-mixed oil/vinegar solution, leaving 1/2-inch headspace.

d) Remove air bubbles and adjust headspace if needed. Wipe rims of jars with a dampened clean paper towel.

73.   Pickled dilled okra

Ingredients

- 7 lbs. small okra pods
- 6 small hot peppers
- 4 teaspoons dill seed
- 8 to 9 garlic cloves
- 2/3 cup canning or pickling salt
- 6 cups water
- 6 cups vinegar (5%)

Yield: About 8 to 9 pints

Directions:

a) Wash and trim okra. Fill hot jars firmly with whole okra, leaving 1/2-inch headspace. Place 1 garlic clove in each jar.

b) Combine salt, hot peppers, dill seed, water, and vinegar in large saucepan and bring to a boil. Pour hot pickling solution over okra, leaving 1/2-inch headspace.

c) Remove air bubbles and adjust headspace if needed. Wipe rims of jars with a dampened clean paper towel.

74. Pickled pearl onions

Ingredients:

- 8 cups peeled white pearl onions
- 5-1/2 cups white vinegar (5%)
- 1 cup water
- 2 teaspoons canning salt
- 2 cups sugar
- 8 teaspoons mustard seed
- 4 teaspoons celery seed

Yield: About 3 to 4 pints

Directions:

a) To peel onions, place a few at a time in a wire-mesh basket or strainer, dip in boiling water for 30 seconds, then remove and place in cold water for 30 seconds. Cut a 1/16th-inch slice from the root end, and then remove the peel and cut 1/16th-inch from the other end of the onion.

b) Combine vinegar, water, salt and sugar in an 8-quart Dutch oven or stockpot. Bring to a boil and boil 3 minutes.

c) Add peeled onions and bring back to a boil. Reduce heat to a simmer and heat until half-cooked (about 5 minutes).

d) Meanwhile, place 2 teaspoons mustard seed and 1 teaspoon celery seed into each empty hot pint jar. Fill with hot onions, leaving 1-inch headspace. Fill with hot pickling liquid, leaving 1/2-inch headspace.

e) Remove air bubbles and adjust headspace if needed. Wipe rims of jars with a dampened clean paper towel.

75. Marinated peppers

Ingredients:

- Bell, Hungarian, banana, or jalapeño
- 4 lbs. firm peppers
- 1 cup bottled lemon juice
- 2 cups white vinegar (5%)
- 1 Tablespoon oregano leaves
- 1 cup olive or salad oil
- 1/2 cup chopped onions
- 2 cloves garlic, quartered (optional)
- 2 Tablespoons prepared horseradish (optional)

Yield: About 9 half-pints

Directions:

a) Select your favorite pepper. Caution: If you select hot peppers, wear plastic or rubber gloves and do not touch your face while handling or cutting hot peppers.

b) Wash, slash two to four slits in each pepper, and blanch in boiling water or blister skins on tough-skinned hot peppers using one of these two methods:

c) Oven or broiler method to blister skins – Place peppers in a hot oven (400°F) or under a broiler for 6 to 8 minutes until skins blister.

d) Range-top method to blister skins – Cover hot burner (either gas or electric) with heavy wire mesh.

e) Place peppers on burner for several minutes until skins blister.

f) After blistering skins, place peppers in a pan and cover with a damp cloth. (This will make peeling the peppers easier.) Cool several minutes; peel of skins. Flatten whole peppers.

g) Mix all remaining ingredients in a saucepan and heat to boiling. Place 1/4 garlic clove (optional) and 1/4 teaspoon salt in each hot half-pint jar or 1/2 teaspoon per pint. Fill hot jars with peppers. Add hot, well-mixed oil/pickling solution over peppers, leaving 1/2-inch headspace.

h) Remove air bubbles and adjust headspace if needed. Wipe rims of jars with a dampened clean paper towel.

76.   Pickled bell peppers

Ingredients:

- 7 lbs. bell peppers
- 3-1/2 cups sugar
- 3 cups vinegar (5%)
- 3 cups water
- 9 cloves garlic
- 4-1/2 teaspoons canning or pickling salt

Yield: About 9 pints

Directions:

a) Wash peppers, cut into quarters, remove cores and seeds, and cut away any blemishes. Slice peppers in strips. Boil sugar, vinegar, and water for 1 minute.

b) Add peppers and bring to a boil. Place 1/2 clove of garlic and 1/4 teaspoon salt in each hot sterile half-pint jar; double the amounts for pint jars.

c) Add pepper strips and cover with hot vinegar mixture, leaving 1/2-inch

77. Pickled hot peppers

Ingredients:

- Hungarian, banana, chile, jalapeño
- 4 lbs. hot long red, green, or yellow peppers
- 3 lbs. sweet red and green peppers, mixed
- 5 cups vinegar (5%)
- 1 cup water
- 4 teaspoons canning or pickling salt
- 2 Tablespoons sugar
- 2 cloves garlic

Yield: About 9 pints

Directions:

a) Caution: Wear plastic or rubber gloves and do not touch your face while handling or cutting hot peppers. If you do not wear gloves, wash hands thoroughly with soap and water before touching your face or eyes.

b) Wash peppers. If small peppers are left whole, slash 2 to 4 slits in each. Quarter large peppers.

c) Blanch in boiling water or blister skins on tough-skinned hot peppers using one of these two methods:

d) Oven or broiler method to blister skins – Place peppers in a hot oven (400°F) or under a broiler for 6 to 8 minutes until skins blister.

e) Range-top method to blister skins – Cover hot burner (either gas or electric) with heavy wire mesh.

f) Place peppers on burner for several minutes until skins blister.

g) After blistering skins, place peppers in a pan and cover with a damp cloth. (This will make peeling the peppers easier.) Cool several minutes; peel of skins. Flatten small peppers. Quarter large peppers. Fill hot jars with peppers, leaving 1/2-inch headspace.

h) Combine and heat other ingredients to boiling and simmer 10 minutes. Remove garlic. Add hot pickling solution over peppers, leaving 1/2-inch headspace.

i) Remove air bubbles and adjust headspace if needed. Wipe rims of jars with a dampened clean paper towel.

78. Pickled jalapeño pepper rings

Ingredients:

- 3 lbs. jalapeño peppers
- 1-1/2 cups pickling lime
- 1-1/2 gallons water
- 7-1/2 cups cider vinegar (5%)
- 1-3/4 cups water
- 2-1/2 Tablespoons canning salt
- 3 Tablespoons celery seed
- 6 Tablespoons mustard seed

Yield: About 6 pint jars

Directions:

a) Caution: Wear plastic or rubber gloves and do not touch your face while handling or cutting hot peppers.

b) Wash peppers well and slice into 1/4-inch thick slices. Discard stem end.

c) Mix 1-1/2 cups pickling lime with 1-1/2 gallons water in a stainless steel, glass or food grade plastic container. Avoid inhaling lime dust while mixing the lime-water solution.

d) Soak pepper slices in the lime water, in refrigerator, for 18 hours, stirring occasionally (12 to 24 hours may be used). Drain lime solution from soaked pepper rings.

e) Rinse peppers gently but thoroughly with water. Cover pepper rings with fresh cold water and soak, in refrigerator, 1 hour. Drain water from peppers. Repeat the rinsing, soaking and draining steps two more times. Drain thoroughly at the end.

f) Place 1 tablespoon mustard seed and 1-1/2 teaspoons celery seed in the bottom of each hot pint jar. Pack drained pepper rings into the jars, leaving 1/2-inch headspace. Bring cider vinegar, 1-3/4 cups water and canning salt to a boil over high heat. Ladle boiling hot brine solution over pepper rings in jars, leaving 1/2-inch headspace.

g) Remove air bubbles and adjust headspace if needed. Wipe rims of jars with a dampened clean paper towel.

79. Pickled yellow pepper rings

Ingredients:

- 2-1/2 to 3 lbs. yellow (banana) peppers
- 2 Tablespoons celery seed
- 4 Tablespoons mustard seed
- 5 cups cider vinegar (5%)
- 1-1/4 cups water
- 5 teaspoons canning salt

Yield: About 4 pint jars

Directions:

a) Wash peppers well and remove stem end; slice peppers into 1/4-inch thick rings. Place 1/2 tablespoon celery seed and 1 tablespoon mustard seed in the bottom of each empty hot pint jar.

b) Fill pepper rings into jars, leaving 1/2-inch head-space. In a 4-quart Dutch oven or saucepan, combine the cider vinegar, water and salt; heat to boiling. Cover pepper rings with boiling pickling liquid, leaving 1/2-inch headspace.

c) Remove air bubbles and adjust headspace if needed. Wipe rims of jars with a dampened clean paper towel.

80. Pickled sweet green tomatoes

Ingredients:

- 10 to 11 lbs. of green tomatoes
- 2 cups sliced onions
- 1/4 cup canning or pickling salt
- 3 cups brown sugar
- 4 cups vinegar (5%)
- 1 Tablespoon mustard seed
- 1 Tablespoon allspice
- 1 Tablespoon celery seed
- 1 Tablespoon whole cloves

Yield: About 9 pints

Directions:

a) Wash and slice tomatoes and onions. Place in bowl, sprinkle with 1/4 cup salt, and let stand 4 to 6 hours. Drain. Heat and stir sugar in vinegar until dissolved.

b) Tie mustard seed, allspice, celery seed, and cloves in a spice bag. Add to vinegar with tomatoes and onions. If needed, add minimum water to cover pieces. Bring to boil and simmer 30 minutes, stirring as needed to prevent burning. Tomatoes should be tender and transparent when properly cooked.

c) Remove spice bag. Fill hot jar with solids and cover with hot pickling solution, leaving 1/2-inch headspace.

d) Remove air bubbles and adjust headspace if needed. Wipe rims of jars with a dampened clean paper towel.

81. Pickled mixed vegetables

Ingredients:

- 4 lbs. of 4- to 5-inch pickling cucumbers
- 2 lbs. peeled and quartered small onions
- 4 cups cut celery (1-inch pieces)
- 2 cups peeled and cut carrots (1/2-inch pieces)
- 2 cups cut sweet red peppers (1/2-inch pieces)
- 2 cups cauliflower flowerets
- 5 cups white vinegar (5%)
- 1/4 cup prepared mustard
- 1/2 cup canning or pickling salt
- 3-1/2 cups sugar
- 3 Tablespoons celery seed
- 2 Tablespoons mustard seed
- 1/2 teaspoons whole cloves
- 1/2 teaspoons ground turmeric

Yield: About 10 pints

Directions:

a) Combine vegetables, cover with 2 inches of cubed or crushed ice, and refrigerate 3 to 4 hours. In 8-quart kettle, combine vinegar and mustard and mix well. Add salt, sugar, celery seed, mustard seed, cloves, turmeric. Bring to a boil. Drain vegetables and add to hot pickling solution.

b) Cover and slowly bring to boil. Drain vegetables but save pickling solution. Fill vegetables in hot sterile pint jars, or hot quarts, leaving 1/2-inch headspace. Add pickling solution, leaving 1/2-inch headspace.

c) Remove air bubbles and adjust headspace if needed. Wipe rims of jars with a dampened clean paper towel.

82. Pickled bread-and-butter zucchini

Ingredients:

- 16 cups fresh zucchini, sliced
- 4 cups onions, thinly sliced
- 1/2 cup canning or pickling salt
- 4 cups white vinegar (5%)
- 2 cups sugar
- 4 Tablespoons mustard seed
- 2 Tablespoons celery seed
- 2 teaspoons ground turmeric

Yield: About 8 to 9 pints

Directions:

a) Cover zucchini and onion slices with 1 inch of water and salt. Let stand 2 hours and drain thoroughly. Combine vinegar, sugar, and spices. Bring to a boil and add zucchini and onions. Simmer 5 minutes and ill hot jars with mixture and pickling solution, leaving 1/2-inch headspace.

b) Remove air bubbles and adjust headspace if needed. Wipe rims of jars with a dampened clean paper towel.

83. Chayote and pear relish

Ingredients:

- 3-1/2 cups peeled, cubed chayote
- 3-1/2 cups peeled, cubed Seckel pears
- 2 cups chopped red bell pepper
- 2 cups chopped yellow bell pepper
- 3 cups chopped onion
- 2 Serrano peppers, chopped
- 2-1/2 cups cider vinegar (5%)
- 1-1/2 cups water
- 1 cup white sugar
- 2 teaspoons canning salt
- 1 teaspoon ground allspice
- 1 teaspoon ground pumpkin pie spice

Yield: About 5 pint jars

Directions:

a) Wash, peel and cut chayote and pears into 1/2-inch cubes, discarding cores and seeds. Chop onions and peppers. Combine vinegar, water, sugar, salt and spices in a Dutch oven or large saucepot. Bring to a boil, stirring to dissolve sugar.

b) Add chopped onions and peppers; return to a boil and boil for 2 minutes, stirring occasionally.

c) Add cubed chayote and pears; return to the boiling point and turn off heat. Fill the hot solids into hot pint jars, leaving 1-inch headspace. Cover with boiling cooking liquid, leaving 1/2-inch headspace.

d) Remove air bubbles and adjust headspace if needed. Wipe rims of jars with a dampened clean paper towel.

84. Piccalilli

Ingredients:

- 6 cups chopped green tomatoes
- 1-1/2 cups chopped sweet red peppers
- 1-1/2 cups chopped green peppers
- 2-1/4 cups chopped onions
- 7-1/2 cups chopped cabbage
- 1/2 cup canning or pickling salt
- 3 Tablespoons whole mixed pickling spice
- 4-1/2 cups vinegar (5%)
- 3 cups brown sugar

Yield: About 9 half-pints

Directions:

a) Wash, chop, and combine vegetables with 1/2 cup salt. Cover with hot water and let stand 12 hours. Drain and press in a clean white cloth to remove all possible liquid. Tie spices loosely in a spice bag and add to combined vinegar and brown sugar and heat to a boil in a sauce pan.

b) Add vegetables and boil gently 30 minutes or until the volume of the mixture is reduced by one-half. Remove spice bag.

c) Fill hot sterile jars, with hot mixture, leaving 1/2-inch headspace.

d) Remove air bubbles and adjust headspace if needed. Wipe rims of jars with a dampened clean paper towel.

85. Pickle relish

Ingredients:

- 3 quarts chopped cucumbers
- 3 cups each of chopped sweet green and red peppers
- 1 cup chopped onions
- 3/4 cup canning or pickling salt
- 4 cups ice
- 8 cups water
- 2 cups sugar
- 4 teaspoons each of mustard seed, turmeric, whole allspice, and whole cloves
- 6 cups white vinegar (5%)

Yield: About 9 pints

Directions:

a) Add cucumbers, peppers, onions, salt, and ice to water and let stand 4 hours. Drain and re-cover vegetables with fresh ice water for another hour. Drain again.

b) Combine spices in a spice or cheesecloth bag. Add spices to sugar and vinegar. Heat to boiling and pour mixture over vegetables.

c) Cover and refrigerate 24 hours. Heat mixture to boiling and ill hot into hot jars, leaving 1/2-inch headspace.

d) Remove air bubbles and adjust headspace if needed. Wipe rims of jars with a dampened clean paper towel.

86. Pickled corn relish

Ingredients:

- 10 cups fresh whole kernel corn
- 2-1/2 cups diced sweet red peppers
- 2-1/2 cups diced sweet green peppers
- 2-1/2 cups chopped celery
- 1-1/4 cups diced onions
- 1-3/4 cups sugar
- 5 cups vinegar (5%)
- 2-1/2 Tablespoons canning or pickling salt
- 2-1/2 teaspoons celery seed
- 2-1/2 Tablespoons dry mustard
- 1-1/4 teaspoons turmeric

Yield: About 9 pints

Directions:

a) Boil ears of corn 5 minutes. Dip in cold water. Cut whole kernels from cob or use six 10-ounce frozen packages of corn.

b) Combine peppers, celery, onions, sugar, vinegar, salt, and celery seed in a saucepan.

c) Bring to boil and simmer 5 minutes, stirring occasionally. Mix mustard and turmeric in 1/2 cup of the simmered mixture. Add this mixture and corn to the hot mixture.

d) Simmer another 5 minutes. Fill hot jars with hot mixture, leaving 1/2-inch headspace.

e) Remove air bubbles and adjust headspace if needed. Wipe rims of jars with a dampened clean paper towel.

87. Pickled green tomato relish

Ingredients:

- 10 lbs. small, hard green tomatoes
- 1-1/2 lbs. red bell peppers
- 1-1/2 lbs. green bell peppers
- 2 lbs. onions
- 1/2 cup canning or pickling salt
- 1-quart water
- 4 cups sugar
- 1-quart vinegar (5%)
- 1/3 cup prepared yellow mustard
- 2 Tablespoons cornstarch

Yield: About 7 to 9 pints

Directions:

a) Wash and coarsely grate or chop tomatoes, peppers, and onions. Dissolve salt in water and pour over vegetables in large kettle.

b) Heat to boiling and simmer 5 minutes. Drain in colander. Return vegetables to kettle.

c) Add sugar, vinegar, mustard, and cornstarch. Stir to mix. Heat to boiling and simmer 5 minutes.

d) Fill hot sterile pint jars with hot relish, leaving 1/2-inch headspace.

e) Remove air bubbles and adjust headspace if needed. Wipe rims of jars with a dampened clean paper towel.

88. Pickled horseradish sauce

Ingredients:

- 2 cups (3/4 lb.) freshly grated horseradish
- 1 cup white vinegar (5%)
- 1/2 teaspoons canning or pickling salt
- 1/4 teaspoons powdered ascorbic acid

Yield: About 2 half-pints

Directions:

a) The pungency of fresh horseradish fades within 1 to 2 months, even when refrigerated. Therefore, make only small quantities at a time.

b) Wash horseradish roots thoroughly and peel of brown outer skin. The peeled roots may be grated in a food processor or cut into small cubes and put through a food grinder.

c) Combine ingredients and ill into sterile jars, leaving 1/4-inch headspace.

d) Seal jars tightly and store in a refrigerator.

89. Pickled pepper-onion relish

Ingredients:

- 6 cups chopped onions
- 3 cups chopped sweet red peppers
- 3 cups chopped green peppers
- 1-1/2 cups sugar
- 6 cups vinegar (5%), preferably white distilled
- 2 Tablespoons canning or pickling salt

Yield: About 9 half-pints

Directions:

a) Wash and chop vegetables. Combine all ingredients and boil gently until mixture thickens and volume is reduced by one-half (about 30 minutes).

b) Fill hot sterile jars with hot relish, leaving 1/2-inch headspace, and seal tightly.

c) Store in refrigerator and use within one month.

90. Spicy jicama relish

Ingredients:

- 9 cups diced jicama
- 1 Tablespoon whole mixed pickling spice
- 1 two-inch stick cinnamon
- 8 cups white vinegar (5%)
- 4 cups sugar
- 2 teaspoons crushed red pepper
- 4 cups diced yellow bell pepper
- 4-1/2 cups diced red bell pepper
- 4 cups chopped onion
- 2 fresh hot peppers

Yield: About 7 pint jars

Directions:

a) Caution: Wear plastic or rubber gloves and do not touch your face while handling or cutting hot peppers. Wash, peel and trim jicama; dice.

b) Place pickling spice and cinnamon on a clean, double-layer, 6-inch-square piece of 100% cotton cheesecloth.

c) Bring corners together and tie with a clean string.

d) In a 4-quart Dutch oven or saucepot, combine pickling spice bag, vinegar, sugar, and crushed red pepper. Bring to boiling, stirring to dissolve sugar. Stir in diced jicama, sweet peppers, onion and fingerhots. Return mixture to boiling.

e) Reduce heat and simmer, covered, over medium-low heat about 25 minutes. Discard spice bag. Fill relish into hot pint jars, leaving 1/2-inch headspace. Cover with hot pickling liquid, leaving 1/2-inch headspace.

f) Remove air bubbles and adjust headspace if needed. Wipe rims of jars with a dampened clean paper towel.

91. Tangy tomatillo relish

Ingredients:

- 12 cups chopped tomatillos
- 3 cups chopped jicama
- 3 cups chopped onion
- 6 cups chopped plum-type tomatoes
- 1-1/2 cups chopped green bell pepper
- 1-1/2 cups chopped red bell pepper
- 1-1/2 cups chopped yellow bell pepper
- 1 cup canning salt
- 2 quarts water
- 6 Tablespoons whole mixed pickling spice
- 1 Tablespoon crushed red pepper flakes (optional)
- 6 cups sugar
- 6-1/2 cups cider vinegar (5%)

Yield: About 6 or 7 pints

Directions:

a) Remove husks from tomatillos and wash well. Peel jicama and onion. Wash all vegetables well before trimming and chopping.

b) Place chopped tomatillos, jicama, onion, tomatoes, and all bell peppers in a 4-quart Dutch oven or saucepot. Dissolve canning salt in water. Pour over prepared vegetables. Heat to boiling; simmer 5 minutes.

c) Drain thoroughly through a cheesecloth-lined strainer (until no more water drips through, about 15 to 20 minutes).

d) Place pickling spice and optional red pepper flakes on a clean, double-layer, 6 inch-square piece

92. No sugar added pickled beets

Ingredients:

- 7 lbs. of 2- to 2-1/2-inch diameter beets
- 4 to 6 onions (2- to 2-1/2-inch diameter), if desired
- 6 cups white vinegar (5 percent)
- 1-1/2 teaspoons canning or pickling salt
- 2 cups Splenda
- 3 cups water
- 2 cinnamon sticks
- 12 whole cloves

Yield: About 8 pints

Directions:

a) Trim of beet tops, leaving 1 inch of stem and roots to prevent bleeding of color. Wash thoroughly. Sort for size.

b) Cover similar sizes together with boiling water and cook until tender (about 25 to

30 minutes). Caution: Drain and discard liquid. Cool beets.

c) Trim of roots and stems and slip of skins. Slice into 1/4-inch slices. Peel, wash and thinly slice onions.

d) Combine vinegar, salt, Splenda®, and 3 cups fresh water in large Dutch oven. Tie cinnamon sticks and cloves in cheesecloth bag and add to vinegar mixture.

e) Bring to a boil. Add beets and onions. Simmer

f) 5 minutes. Remove spice bag. Fill hot beets and onion slices into hot pint jars, leaving 1/2-inch headspace. Cover with boiling vinegar solution, leaving 1/2-inch headspace.

g) Remove air bubbles and adjust headspace if needed. Wipe rims of jars with a dampened clean paper towel.

93. Sweet pickle cucumber

Ingredients:

- 3-1/2 lbs. of pickling cucumbers
- boiling water to cover sliced cucumbers
- 4 cups cider vinegar (5%)
- 1 cup water
- 3 cups Splenda®
- 1 Tablespoon canning salt
- 1 Tablespoon mustard seed
- 1 Tablespoon whole allspice
- 1 Tablespoon celery seed
- 4 one-inch cinnamon sticks

Yield: About 4 or 5 pint jars

Directions:

a) Wash cucumbers. Slice 1/16th-inch of the blossom ends and discard. Slice cucumbers into 1/4-inch thick slices.

Pour boiling water over the cucumber slices and let stand 5 to 10 minutes.

b) Drain of the hot water and pour cold water over the cucumbers. Let cold water run continuously over the cucumber slices, or change water frequently until cucumbers are cooled. Drain slices well.

c) Mix vinegar, 1 cup water, Splenda® and all spices in a 10-quart Dutch oven or stockpot. Bring to a boil. Add drained cucumber slices carefully to the boiling liquid and return to a boil.

d) Place one cinnamon stick in each empty hot jar, if desired. Fill hot pickle slices into hot pint jars, leaving 1/2-inch headspace. Cover with boiling pickling brine, leaving 1/2-inch headspace.

e) Remove air bubbles and adjust headspace if needed. Wipe rims of jars with a dampened clean paper towel.

94. Sliced dill pickles

Ingredients:

- 4 lbs. (3- to 5-inch) pickling cucumbers
- 6 cups vinegar (5%)
- 6 cups sugar
- 2 Tablespoons canning or pickling salt
- 1-1/2 teaspoons celery seed
- 1-1/2 teaspoons mustard seed
- 2 large onions, thinly sliced
- 8 heads fresh dill

Yield: About 8 pints

Directions:

a) Wash cucumbers. Cut 1/16-inch slice of blossom end and discard. Cut cucumbers in 1/4-inch slices. Combine vinegar, sugar, salt, celery, and mustard seeds in large saucepan. Bring mixture to boiling.

b) Place 2 slices of onion and 1/2 dill head on bottom of each hot pint jar. Fill hot jars with cucumber slices, leaving 1/2-inch headspace.

c) Add 1 slice of onion and 1/2 dill head on top. Pour hot pickling solution over cucumbers, leaving 1/4-inch headspace.

d) Remove air bubbles and adjust headspace if needed. Wipe rims of jars with a dampened clean paper towel.

95. Sliced sweet pickles

Ingredients:

- 4 lbs. (3- to 4-inch) pickling cucumbers

Brining solution:

- 1-quart distilled white vinegar (5%)
- 1 Tablespoon canning or pickling salt
- 1 Tablespoon mustard seed
- 1/2 cup sugar

Canning syrup:

- 1-2/3 cups distilled white vinegar (5%)
- 3 cups sugar
- 1 Tablespoon whole allspice
- 2-1/4 teaspoons celery seed

Yield: About 4 to 5 pints

Directions:

a) Wash cucumbers and cut 1/16 inch of blossom end, and discard. Cut cucumbers into 1/4-inch slices. Combine all ingredients for canning syrup in a saucepan and bring to boiling. Keep syrup hot until used.

b) In a large kettle, mix the ingredients for the brining solution. Add the cut cucumbers, cover, and simmer until the cucumbers change color from bright to dull green (about 5 to 7 minutes). Drain the cucumber slices.

c) Fill hot jars, and cover with hot canning syrup leaving 1/2-inch headspace.

d) Remove air bubbles and adjust headspace if needed. Wipe rims of jars with a dampened clean paper towel.

96. Lemon & Dill Kraut

Ingredients:

- 1 head firm white cabbage, finely sliced
- 2 to 3 teaspoons sea salt (1.5%)
- 2 tablespoons lemon juice
- 1 tablespoon dried dill
- 2 -3 cloves garlic, finely grated

Directions:

a) Wash your cabbage and reserve one of the outer leaves to tuck in top of your kraut.
b) Cut the cabbage in quarters, remove the core, and shred finely. Follow the directions above for normal sauerkraut, adding the lemon juice and the dried dill with the salt.
c) Squeeze and massage the cabbage until it is glistening and there is a small pool of liquid in the bottom of the bowl, then mix in the garlic.

97. Chinese Kimchi

Ingredients:

- 1 head of napa or Chinese cabbage, chopped
- 3 carrots, grated
- 1 large daikon radish, grated or a cup of small red radishes, finely sliced
- 1 large onion, chopped
- 1/4 cup of dulse or nori seaweed flakes
- 1 tablespoon chile pepper flakes
- 1 tablespoon minced garlic
- 1 tablespoon minced fresh ginger
- 1 tablespoon sesame seeds
- 1 tablespoon sugar
- 2 teaspoons good quality sea salt
- 1 teaspoon of fish sauce

Directions:

a) Simply mix all the ingredients together in a large bowl and let it sit for 30 minutes.
b) Pack the mixture into a large glass mason jar or 2 smaller jars. Press it down firmly.
c) Top with a water filled Ziploc bag to keep oxygen out and keep the veggies submerged under the brine.
d) Put the lid on loosely and set aside to ferment for at least 3 days. Taste it after 3 days and decide whether it tastes sour enough. It's a matter of personal taste so just keep trying it until you like it!
e) Once you are happy with the flavour you can store the kimchi in the fridge where it will keep happily for months, if it lasts that long!!

98. Fermented Carrot Sticks

Ingredients:

- 6 organic carrots, washed and cut into sticks
- 2 % brine solution (20g sea salt dissolved in 1 litre filtered water)
- Few garlic cloves, lemon slices, black peppercorns, bay leaves or dill

Directions:

a) Pack the carrots tightly into a clean 1 litre glass jar, along with any other seasoning from the ingredients list. Pour the brine over to within 2.5 cm of the top of the jar.
b) If the carrots are floating above the level of liquid, then you can use a Ziploc bag filled with brine to weigh them down and keep them safely submerged.
c) Leave to ferment at room temperature, out of direct sunlight, for at least a week, but preferably two weeks. The brine will start to look cloudy which indicates fermentation is proceeding normally. You should also see some bubbles if you gently shake the jar.
d) Once you are happy with the flavour and texture then move them to the fridge, where they will keep happily for a few months!

99. Carrots with an Indian Twist

(Makes 1 litre jar)

Ingredients:

- 1 kg carrots, peeled and grated
- 1 knob fresh ginger, peeled and grated
- 2 tsp chili flakes
- 2 tsp fenugreek
- 2 tsp mustard seed
- 1 tsp ground turmeric
- 1 tablespoon sea salt

Directions:

a) Place the carrots in a bowl and sprinkle with the sea salt.
b) Squeeze and massage the mixture to release some brine. The carrots should start to wilt and become wet.
c) Add the spices and mix together using a wooden spoon, not your hands or they will be stained orange by the turmeric!
d) Pack the mixture into a clean 1 litre glass jar, pressing each handful down firmly to ensure no air is trapped. Leave 2.5cm headspace at the top of the jar and make sure the carrots are completely submerged under the brine.
e) Close the lid and allow to ferment for 5 to 7 days at room temperature.
f) Store the jar in the fridge and use within 6 months.

100.   Radish Bombs

(Makes 1 litre jar)

Ingredients:

- 400g radishes, tops trimmed
- 1 or 2 tsp pickling spice or fennel
- 15g/1 tablespoon sea salt
- 10g/2 tsp caster sugar
- 1 litre filtered water
- 1 red onion sliced or 5 spring onions
- 3 slices fresh ginger
- 2 or 3 large slices of lemon
- 3 or 4 garlic cloves, smashed
- 1 tsp or more dried chili flakes, depending how hot you like it

Directions:

a) Make the brine by dissolving the sea salt and sugar in a jug. Wash your glass jar in hot soapy water and rinse it well to remove any soap residues.

b) Put the spices in the bottom of the jar, then add the vegetables, finishing with the lemon slices on top. Pour the brine over until everything is completely submerged. Cover with a large cabbage leaf or Ziploc bag filled with extra brine to keep everything under the brine.

c) Loosely close the jar and leave somewhere cool and out of direct sunlight for 7 to 12 days. I tend to put mine in the garage since the sulphurous pong can be quite overpowering and you may get complaints from family members!

d) Taste them after 7 days and if they are sour enough for you then transfer them to the fridge where they will keep for around 6 months.

e) If not sour enough then leave them another 4 or 5 days.

f) Keep any excess brine and use it in salad dressings, its teeming with probiotics!!

CONCLUSION

Pickles and sauerkraut might not be the first examples that jump to mind when you think of health foods. But a growing body of research shows that a diet that includes a regular intake of fermented foods can bring benefits.

Fermented foods are preserved using an age-old process that not only boosts the food's shelf life and nutritional value but can give your body a dose of healthful probiotics — live microorganisms crucial to good digestion.

www.ingramcontent.com/pod-product-compliance
Lightning Source LLC
Chambersburg PA
CBHW051704160426
43209CB00004B/1016